STRONG WOMAN, SMALL POTATO

My Story of Addiction and Recovery

Charlene Kodimer with Gina Raith

STRONG WOMAN, SMALL POTATO

My Story of Addiction and Recovery

ISBN 9-798993-62050-3 (paperback)

ISBN 9-798993-62051-0 (ebook)

Front + Back Cover + About the Author + Coming Soon photos by Lelah Nichol
www.markthemomentbayarea.com

And acceptance is the answer to all my problems today.

Wilson, B. (1955). Alcoholic Anonymous: The Story of How More Than One Hundred Men Recovered from Alcoholism ("*The Big Book").*

DEDICATION

This book is dedicated to Dana Horton, my therapist, friend and mentor who has always been there for me … on occasion.

It's also dedicated to my brother who, after reading this book, knocked the wind out of me when he declared it perfect. He brought tears to my eyes, and I'm so proud to call him my brother.

TABLE OF CONTENTS

PREFACE

What follows is the gift that sobriety and Parkinson's gave me: the voice to finally say all of this. It took eight decades to find myself, but here I am. These pieces are based on my admittedly flawed memory. I've changed most names, including the names of the rehab programs I attended. I'm not an expert; if you're struggling, please get professional help. My stories are not necessarily chronological, but rather unconventional, like me. I weave in what I hope to be inspirational shares. Thanks for indulging me. Sharing is caring, and sharing pain and the promise of connection is bold—dare I say YAM-ISH (to be defined herein).

Trigger warning; these pages address sensitive topics including mental illness, addiction, suicide, family violence, sex, eating disorders, self-harm, trauma, disease, aging and its indignities.

Enter at your own risk.

1. TO MARKET WE GO: CHOOSE WISELY

In the summer of 2005, my mother, Dorothy Kodimer, and I headed to Gelson's Market. It was a quintessential sunny morning in Century City. It was also one of my last vivid outings with her before she died. The store smelled of bleach, fresh flowers and cardboard boxes. I was intimately familiar with this olfactory mélange because of my family-owned grocery stores (called ABC) in South Central Los Angeles. We were grocery people, so trips to the market were not especially extraordinary. What *was* extraordinary was my mother's unwavering message that day—the embedded, ever-present message she broadcast from my cradle to her grave. She was nothing if not consistent.

We were in the produce section when I reached for a large potato. She was mortified. It was just a potato, but to her, it symbolized every excess I wasn't allowed to want. And to me, it echoed every message I'd ever absorbed: don't reach for too much.

"How can you possibly choose a large potato?" she hissed. "It's practically a yam!"

And here's where the real message lodged itself in my amygdala and cemented into my bones: How could I possibly have the gall to reach for a large potato—much less a large life?

God forbid I should want butter, sour cream, and chives on that potato—that would be just cause to put me up for adoption. But I was 60, not exactly a prime candidate for rehoming.

This mother-daughter exchange was emblematic of my life: my mother systematically squeezed the life force out of me, one microaggression at a time. She didn't act alone. My cold-hearted father helped her. Consequently, I became an addict, a depressive and an obsessive—the full menu of dysfunction.

And yet, here I am, writing about it.

From the time I was in utero until that morning in the market, my mother left me wanting more. Always more. More potatoes, more condiments, more love.

She was a dyed-in-the-wool restrictive, though, so "more" was never in her vocabulary.

And so I became me: hungry at birth, hungry for everything—especially love.

2. WILD HORSES AND ME

One of my earliest memories, from our first “starter” home as a family, is of the wallpaper in my bedroom. It was filled with horses—horses running, legs extended, manes windswept, eyes wild and free. Any three-year-old girl in her right mind would have counted herself lucky to fall asleep surrounded by such majestic beauty.

And it was all good—until my parents turned off the light.

"Nighty night," one of them would whisper, tiptoeing backwards, leaving my door one inch ajar, as if that narrow beam of hallway light could fend off what was to come.

Every night, despite my best efforts, those damn horses would not stay put. As soon as I drifted off, I’d startle awake, bolt upright, heart pounding. And there they were—leaping off the wall, stampeding toward me.

In panic, I’d hurl myself out of bed and sprint down the hall like my life depended on it, which in my young mind, it did. I’d launch myself—a human torpedo—into the middle of my parents’ king-sized bed. Come to think of it, there was plenty of room between them. In bed. And in life.

I’d nestle in, a piece of nondescript deli meat between two slices of white bread. The warmth of their skin, the softness of their breath, their pajamas—enveloped me. Despite the nightly terror, those rescue missions were everything. In those moments, I felt safe. I felt loved.

Like all good things, it didn't last. Two years later, we moved. The horses stayed behind. So did the snuggles.

It would be a very long time before I felt safely held again.

3. THE ORIGIN STORY OF THE STRONG WOMAN WITH A SMALL POTATO *or... How I Met My First Therapist ... or... Memories of My Mother*

Mother Dorothy was the Queen of Small Portions. "More please" was not in her vocabulary. She never experienced being full, overindulging, or having too much. She gained exactly seven pounds while pregnant with me and wore that fact like a medal. This was L.A. after all. Her parenting motto (having skipped all the books) was simple: *I'm to be the center of attention, and you shall not eclipse me.* As her only daughter, I obliged.

You've heard the phrase "canary in the coal mine"? The dogs of my childhood were my canaries. I should have paid more attention to how she treated them. The dominant emotion she displayed toward her dogs was callousness. Her *modus operandi*: when in doubt, put them out. Not just outside when they were inconvenient—but out, and down. Forever.

God knows what she thought of me, the noisy, needy little creature who arrived to upend her curated, crumb-free life where nothing was out of place. Ever. The one thing we could count on in her orbit was a flashing red light. No green lights, no thriving—just controlling, contorting, contracting.

She relaxed by cleaning out her drawers (the ones in her bureau, not her underwear). She whipped those drawers into shape, early and often. She spent more time with her drawers than her friends. Or her family. Or her dogs.

One of her many faux-furry companions was an adorable black poodle named Jeremy. When he broke his hind leg on the stairs, my mother's solution was to have him put down. No tears. Just a new poodle—Georgie. Then Georgie bit the dust, and Bobbie arrived. Her dogs were for show, not for love. Kind of like her children.

I'm surprised she didn't cash me in when I started to disappoint her. Around my tenth birthday, she likely realized she'd given birth to a Ford Comet, not the Mercedes that hewed to her aesthetic. Mercifully, around that time, we got a family dog—a Springer spaniel named Freckles. He became my therapist.

We had just moved from our starter home in Liemert Park to a newly constructed suburb in Cheviot Hills. My brother Jacob and I were still not allowed to enter the kitchen, much less touch the furniture. There was no reclining on couches, watching movies, eating popcorn. We basically lived in a museum. Mother was the Statue in Chief. She even ran the faucet when she used the bathroom—so no one would hear her pee. Bodily functions were regarded as indecent. I don't remember her lounging in the common areas. She didn't cook, didn't change diapers (there was always a maid for that) and she certainly didn't walk her precious poodles.

The upside of her absence? I got to sneak into our modern kitchen and plop down on the cold, spotless floor beside Freckles. He was an excellent listener, even though every day he heard the same lament: "I live in a joyless house."

Then one day, Freckles was gone.

No explanation. I could only assume he'd been given away for being too messy. Or too bothersome. Or both. She never told me whether he'd been put down—or why. After that, I feared for my own life. Like Freckles, I came with fallout. I broke things inadvertently. Surely, my days were numbered. My mother could have written *How to Disappear Your Dog (or Daughter) in Three Easy Steps.*

Step one: Control and restrict portions. (She counted the dogs' kibble. I am not kidding.) I was allotted one small potato and three ounces of beef for dinner. A surefire recipe for anorexia. It worked. I learned from the OG. Dorothy—

yes, and her little dog too—had anorexia long before it made it into the DSM.

Step two: Make everyone feel small, inconsequential, and insignificant. If she had to starve and take up less space, so did everyone else. The house was spacious, but she made it feel tiny, claustrophobic. The rest of us, dogs included, had nowhere to hide.

Step three: Judge and hyper-scrutinize everything—especially my food choices. I was always doing something wrong. Clothes. Friends. Activities. But mostly, food. All day, every day.

Her favorite words? *DON'T*, *CAN'T*, and *NO*. She was determined to yank the life force out of me. She dressed me in doll-like outfits inappropriate for the playground. It was better, in her eyes, to be prim, proper, and presentable than to *commit child*. My mother would've preferred a drawer to a daughter. The drawers didn't talk back. They didn't cry, mess up the furniture or eat carbs.

My life's work since surviving Dorothy has been to swap out that sanctioned small potato for a big one—of my choosing. Without compunction.

My memories of her include, but are not limited to, the time we were walking in the park and I put my arm around her. "Don't do that!" she snapped. "What will people say?"

Or the day we sat in her OB-GYN's waiting room, and she saw a woman wrangling her toddlers. "I wonder what it would be like to be a grandmother," she mused aloud. By then, my brother had one daughter. I reminded her she *was* a grandmother. She blinked. "Oh. I forgot."

She forgot.

Her failure to register the fact that other sentient beings—dogs, daughter, grandchild—depended on her to be a loving presence is the defining theme of my origin story. Like the puppies, I needed an advocate. Fending for ourselves was, and is, overrated—a truth I processed at length with Freckles.

Her last poodle, Bobbie, was "adopted" (read: rescued) by my beloved cousin Hannah. "Free at last!" I imagined Bobbie bark-thinking as he bounded out of our joyless home and into her arms. Years later, when he started peeing on Hannah's carpet, she simply cleaned it up. It never crossed her mind—or her heart—to put him down for being imperfect. Thanks to Hannah, Bobbie got a happy ending.

I'm still working on mine.

4. SHARING IS CARING

2018

When I was growing up, I had to share a bathroom with my brother. To describe him as emotionally constipated would be unkind (and maybe too on the nose), but there it is. And maybe I was, too.

I would lock the door so he couldn't get in. I would use up all the hot water so he couldn't take a shower. I wasn't doing anything he hadn't done to me, but still—let's just say I wasn't winning any *Sister of the Year* awards. He reminded me of that at every turn … until recently.

We've mended fences, and for that I'm grateful.

Now, at 73, with the benefit of life's rearview mirror, I know the best revenge is living well. We women often forget that. We don't have to be a dumpster fire, drawn to drama and clinging to trauma. We've got this.

These days, I have two bathrooms to myself. I drift from one to the next like a queen inspecting her kingdom, pausing now and then to gaze in the mirror and recite Louise Hay affirmations.

All of which is to say: Stuart Smalley has nothing on me.

And yet, reports from those who know me (starting with me) confirm I still struggle with sharing.

As a diabetic—no newsflash here—I have cravings. Sugar is my North Star. I want all of it. I've never said: *Just a cookie, thanks.* Or: *One scoop of ice cream, please.* You get the gist.

One was never enough for this diabetic diva.

I think it started with those damn Prell commercials. Some svelte, slow-motion goddess (Christie Brinkley, maybe, or her shiny-haired cousin) would sway her voluminous mane like it had its own wind machine, while I sat there with my stringy, dull mop, trapped in comparison mode.

We didn't have a 12-step program for girls with tragic hair, so I muddled through alone—not sharing.

I felt *less than*. And when you feel less than, you want *more, please*. More sugar. More praise. More shimmer. More love.

My scarcity mindset shifted glacially through the years.

I genuinely want my brother to be happy now. To be whole. To have an endless stream of hot water for the rest of his days.

That, I'm told, is progress.

I also want him to know I care now—and that I cared then—even if I couldn't show it at the time.

5. NO FAILING ALLOWED

As a kid, I wasn't allowed to step foot in my mother's kitchen to make a sandwich. She assumed I'd screw it up. And—let's be honest—she wasn't entirely wrong.

Anytime I tried to stretch or try something new, she stepped in. It was more expedient for her to do it herself. She didn't want to be disappointed in me, so she didn't give me the chance to disappoint her.

Here's what I've come to understand: Children become competent by failing. We build resilience by making mistakes, by burning the toast, spilling the milk and trying again.

I didn't get that shot.

Some might call her a "snowplow parent"—clearing obstacles, smoothing the path. But that's not quite right. She didn't pave the way for me. She just *stepped out of the way*, emotionally speaking. She outsourced most parenting duties and maintained control from a distance.

I'm no expert, but here's what I've come to understand from the inside: being semi-ignored and constantly underestimated turned me into an adult governed by the "F" word—fear.

And no wonder. As soon as I escaped that house—far from her kitchen and her rules—I failed. Hard. Epically.

But failure, it turns out, was the beginning of something better. I just didn't know it.

6. HIGH HIGHS AND LOW LOWS

I reached my social zenith in third grade and rode that glorious wave of popularity until I was twelve. I was a star—or at least I felt like one. Latency was good to me.

It all started in Miss Baron's class. I was the new kid on the block—awkward, alone, freshly transferred. I didn't know a soul and was still comfy in my shell, drifting along unnoticed, thank you very much. But Miss Baron broke that spell. She gave me the first gold star of the semester for *Outstanding Student*. I was finally seen. There were whispers among my classmates: *Who's that? Is she new? Where did she come from?*

For the first time in my life, this eight-year-old wannabe diva felt noticed. A veritable mini-celebrity. From that day forward, I was in. I had friends, playmates, lunch buddies. Everyone knew my name. They called me Charky.

Of course, there were a few bumps. One time I got hit by a car and showed up to school with a cast and crutches. Kids can be cruel—anything different is open season. But it didn't last. I bounced back and kept my crown.

Fifth and sixth grade were even better. I retained my status as Charky and became determined to stay on top. When Valentine's Day came around, I secretly sent myself over a hundred cards. I was a winner, dammit.

By junior high, I had so many accolades it made my head spin. Class president. Lower school princess. A sought-after hottie. I had more boyfriends than I could count, but my favorite was Marty. Had I married him, he might've spared me a lot of grief. We broke up in seventh grade. Then along came Jeff. Foolishly, I let him feel me up—and suddenly I was the talk of the entire school. Humiliated and ashamed, I swore off boys until college.

The summer after seventh grade, I went to Camp Hess Kramer, where I was once again an unknown-quantity-turned-hot commodity. Kids lined up to be on my team. By eighth grade, I was a straight-A student, unstoppable—or so I thought.

Then came the crash.

Apex, have you met Cliff?

Depression overtook me overnight. A black cloud settled over everything. My chest felt like it was caving in. No more Charky. No more anything. What my father called *laziness* was not just hormones, it turned out, but rather mental illness. He should have known better. It didn't go away. It didn't abate. I felt like a caged animal—and the cage was pitch black.

What I couldn't have known then was that I'd wrestle with depression for most of my life.

Decades later, I had a Christmas lunch with my friend Barbara. "You can't go on like this," she said in her no-bullshit voice (which all good friends should have). I listened—like I always did with Barbara—and a week later I found a therapist, who connected me with a psychiatrist.

After many rounds of trial-and-error meds, I was prescribed an antipsychotic called Risperdal. It worked. This little miracle of modern medicine gave me seventeen solid years of freedom from depression. For that blessed era, I woke up happy. I even walked the Los Angeles Marathon—not as punishment, but as empowerment.

But then the drug stopped working. Just like that.

Faux Apex, meet New Cliff.

I plunged into a deep depression and wanted to die. Basic tasks became impossible. I saw doctor after doctor. No one had answers. I became unglued. Disillusioned. And to complete Act Two, I relapsed on opiates.

Eventually, I found my way back to sobriety. But the miracle pill has eluded me ever since.

Still, I like to believe the miracle might be now. Maybe I've crafted it myself—by cherishing the highest of highs (thank you Miss Baron) and surviving the lowest of lows.

7. CHARKY, I HARDLY KNEW YE

After peaking in latency—when life was easy and I reigned supreme, to the extent an elementary school All-American Jew nicknamed Charky can—the earth quietly shifted on its axis.

I didn't see it coming. No one does. I certainly didn't sign up in eighth grade for a subtle but crushing depression that would crater me overnight. But that's exactly what happened.

Charky, I hardly knew ye.

My once-popular persona, my confident alt-ego, retreated and went to ground. I withdrew, questioned my worth, and drifted alone lost at the bottom of some emotional ocean.

My goal became invisibility, especially in those harrowing, upscale L.A. middle-school hallways teeming with Gloria Vanderbilt jeans and perfectly feathered hair. (Not mine, of course.)

I stayed depressed for the better part of a decade. I distinctly remember that two people noticed. They called me on my vanishing act.

Mr. Moss, my Sunday school teacher when I was fifteen, not only saw me but saw right through me.

“How are you doing, Charlene? It seems like something’s changed.”

He wasn’t really asking: it was an observation in disguise.

I don’t recall exactly what I said (there was no right answer), but whatever it was, it was enough to mollify him. He moved on to the next adolescent basket case, gaze averted. Mission accomplished.

Years later, in college, a woman who had known me in grammar school approached me at a party. She’d had a couple of drinks, and her filter had been pulled.

“What happened to you?” she asked bluntly. “You’re different. You’re not the wonderful, alive girl I used to know.”

As much as it stung, I knew what she meant.

My Charky-self was irrefutably gone.

My response, once again, didn’t matter—because I was still hiding.

I was so deft at hiding, in fact, that I did it for the next forty years. Give or take.

8. A CHILD (NOT) RAISING CHILDREN

Through decades of therapy, I've come to understand that my mother never grew up. Rather, she related to my older brother, Jacob, and me as a child herself.

We were her dolls—Ken and Barbie—raised in a dollhouse with her doll dogs. Our inconvenient emotions had no place in the curated set she called home. Anger would have clashed with the fabric.

It still animates my words on the page. It still lives in my dark heart—a heart that knows the truth but can't quite reconcile it, can't fully let it go. I long to be free.

Free from her limitations.

Free from her failures.

Free from the daily cascade of judgments and the thousand tiny cuts that left their mark on my soul.

She was a child, I remind myself.

I repeat it like a mantra, carving a path to forgiveness.

I've done my work.

And I often wonder how it might have turned out—if only she had done hers.

9. FROM POPCORN TO PILL-POPPING

My introduction to the world of eating disorders was my mother's restrictive eating when I was in her womb. She told anyone who would listen about her newly minted skill: *disordered eating whilst gestating.*

By that measure, I was anorexic from conception. Once expelled from her womb, I yearned for breastmilk, but she would have none of that. And as a result, I would have none of that. It was bottled Similac and nothing else for this un-thriving infant. To my mother's way of thinking, breastfeeding—all that slurping—was untidy and inconvenient.

I somehow managed to have an unremarkable elementary-school span. I ate, played, sometimes in the mud, and got in trouble, on repeat.

Cut to me at age twelve, though, entering the brave new world of debilitating middle-school depression. As mentioned, I flipped the switch overnight from lively, bright and outgoing preteen to sullen, somnambulist adolescent whose most honed skill was looking at the ground. At some point, eating actual food became optional—and the one thing I could control.

This realization struck me like lightning a couple years later while staring into a bag of popcorn at my new high school in Culver City: *I could eat one bag of popcorn for lunch, and nothing else, until my senior year.* Despite its wholesale lack of nutritional content, popcorn became my only nourishment, day-in, day-out. I essentially swapped out friends for popcorn. Well, that's not exactly true; popcorn was not my only friend.

I had two besties: Emily and Grace. They were cheerleaders, on the student council and in elite social clubs. Social clubs were a thing in the sixties. I was in a social club as well, but it was decidedly not "elite." Emily and Grace struggled with their weight. I'm sure it had nothing to do with our options, which ranged from Chef Boyardee to SpaghettiOs to the wonders of Jell-O, not to mention whole milk with all the hormones, thanks, and frozen TV dinners. I stayed away from Hungry Man and Stouffers.

Emily managed her weight by taking amphetamines. I thought that was a nifty thing to do, so I periodically filched uppers from her backpack. I should have noted at that point that popping pills was far too easy for me. Instead, I catalogued my new habit as one of survival. I was also keenly harboring a secret under my loose-fitting clothes: my weight teetered between 100 and 105 pounds, and I couldn't get thin enough.

I gave up my popcorn diet when I entered college at UC Berkeley and turned to drugs to keep my despondence at bay. Pop, pop, pop—stolen, prescribed (mine or someone else's)—I was not particular. Seminally, my lovely internist steered me to Percodan, an opioid, to relieve my cramps. It didn't help the menstrual cramps I didn't have, but it sure helped my depression. It also tamped down my appetite. I was light years ahead of Ozempic, just sayin'.

Some days, I'd limit myself to one slice of Kraft American cheese. What was left of me, having winnowed myself down to 96 pounds by the end of freshman year, was often loathe to leave my residence hall for fear of others thinking: *Look how fat she is.* I could count the ribs on my back which resembled a xylophone. Ding. Ding. Dead inside.

The mind, once weaponized, can seriously compromise sound decision-making. Mine was no exception. Over time, I leaned into my drug of choice, Valium, rationalizing that it was better to sleep than perpetually bounce around, unfocused. Never mind the addiction properties of my legit script! Opioids were not hard to come by back in the day and were practically state sponsored. We've all seen *Mad Men.* The print ads were legion. It was easier to keep us medicated than to deal with us, after all.

My parents wanted me to be a teacher, a nurse or a secretary, none of which interested me. My interests, however, took a backseat to my parents' expectations, so (un)naturally I became a teacher. Deep down, I wanted to be a journalist. Without warning them, I enrolled in USC's journalism school. By the time I got to USC, I had effectively swapped out three square meals a day for Valium. Too much Valium, hordes in fact. I always had my yellow and blue buddies with me, along with the illusion that they would get me through anything. But that was a misguided falsehood. I was so afraid of life, my feelings, everything. To be seen ran the risk of disappointing my parents. So, I stayed invisible.

I floated in an anorexic haze for 20 years before snapping out of it in 1983 when driving by a McDonald's. *I wonder what that would taste like in my mouth?* I ordered a Big Mac, fries and a Diet Coke—of course a Diet Coke. The Diet Coke was the vestige of my anorexia; the Big Mac was the harbinger to my new eating disorder.

Apparently, it was crucial to carry out the dye that was cast in my DNA. While I can't blame Mother entirely, I can cast aspersions. She made me. The New Me, at age 34, loved food without limit. I packed on the pounds.

There was a new Char in town.

10. NOT DADDY'S GIRL

I was never comfortable in the same room as my father. In middle school, during my first major depressive dip, he called me fat and lazy. He told me, repeatedly and with authority, that I'd have to become a teacher—because I wasn't smart or industrious enough to be a journalist. He should know, of course. He knew everything.

If he had said just *one* kind thing—anything to make me feel seen or loved—it might've changed the arc of our story. Instead, he doused my dreams at every turn.

As I got older, I spent time with him out of a futile sense of obligation. The truth? I couldn't wait to leave.

When Dad's denouement finally came, he lay in bed day after day. He could no longer walk, eat, swallow, or go to the bathroom. All he could do was listen to talk radio. That was his final act—the only thing his Parkinson's allowed.

It was gutting to watch this once-commanding man reduced to a passive listener. He had gone from meeting presidents—Reagan, Ford—to being fed through a tube, his eyes distant and unfocused. He was halfway gone, but not yet dead.

Visiting him in the hospital felt like visiting a stranger. Who *was* this man? He'd been on the planet 77 years, and I hardly knew him. We were so different.

He clung to each shallow breath before finally succumbing in a hospital bed, alone. Pneumonia finished what Parkinson's started.

I wish I could say I grieved. But there was no relationship to mourn. No love lost. He was a brilliant businessman—and a terrible father. Narcissistic, egocentric, and always right, he had a million ways to make his only daughter feel invisible.

I couldn't empathize with my father's pain—not then. Not until Parkinson's came for me.

Now, with death drawing closer each day (dramatic, but true), I can finally understand his fear. I *hope* for a peaceful end—pain-free, with dignity. That hope, of course, is at war with my reality.

My depression has lasted for decades. The physical and emotional agony colors everything. And still, I've always thought I'd hang around to see how it ends. Some days, I'm not so sure.

My father wouldn't approve of that. I still hear him: *No throwing in the towel! Buck up! Handle it!*

If I had one more chance to speak with him, I'd tell him this:

I tried. I really did. I wanted to be somebody. Somebody successful. Somebody loved by her father.

But that wasn't meant to be.

I'd remind him that when a child doesn't feel important to their parents, it becomes almost impossible to feel important in the world.

But I know exactly how that conversation would end.

He'd talk over me, wave it all away, and remind me—once again—that *Father knows best.*

11. THE LITTLE TRAIN THAT COULDN'T

We will not regret the past nor wish to shut the door on it. We will contemplate the word serenity and we will know peace.
—Alcoholics Anonymous: The Big Book, Bill Wilson (1955)

A couple decades of my life—from age 17 to 37—you know, the years after high school but before rehab—are, frankly, a blur. Those so-called "formative years," the ones promised to be about self-discovery and personal growth? Mine didn't read like the brochure.

I vividly recall sitting on the steps of my dorm at UC Berkeley, age 17, wondering what in the world I was doing there. I had just clawed my way out of my First Great Depression, which began like clockwork at 13—the official starting bell of adolescence. As a teen, I was trained not to eat, not to pout and not to take up space. Thanks to Mother, I didn't stand a chance at happiness.

Still, I made it through. College at Berkeley. Grad school at Cal State Northridge. Armed with degrees but lacking drive, direction. With no self-initiative, the engine stalled. The little train that couldn't.

I numbed so I wouldn't feel, then numbed because I didn't feel like feeling. (See what I did there?)

The next twenty years were lost to drugs.

At 38, I reported to rehab for the first time. It was my wobbly baby step toward what would become the journey of a lifetime—toward sobriety and Self.

Then came my Second Great Depression, five years later. This time, medications were an option—and, hallelujah, some of them worked. I entered what I now call my *med-trance*: 17 years of chemically assisted unproductive glee. It's good to be gone—until it isn't.

Eventually, I relapsed on pharmaceuticals. The party was over. And that was terrifying.

I overdosed and returned to rehab—round two.

At least I failed faster the second time.

I emerged from that blur with just me, myself and I.

Detoxing alone in Encino is not for the faint of heart.

After two months at a rehab in Northern California, I landed at an SLE (sober living environment) in Tiburon, which led to another (world's shortest) relapse. (To my credit.)

Rehab stint number three took place in Petaluma, California. Because why not get clean in wine country—what could possibly go wrong?

There, I learned the hard truth: you can't go home again. But you *can* come full circle. And when I did, I arrived back at myself.

Still lowercase "self." But I was learning to feel safe with me.

And that was no small thing. Because what came later would test me in ways I could never have imagined.

12. WHEN TOO MUCH WAS NEVER ENOUGH

It was a day like any other. I sat alone in my dim apartment, flipping absently through an entertainment rag—*People*, maybe *Star*. Beside me, a Waterford glass of Harvey's Bristol Cream—the sweet sherry my father favored—went down in sips, then gulps. A dozen Valium followed. My solitude was deep, drugged, and uninterrupted. Until the phone rang.

The phone that never rang.

One ringy-dingy, two ringy-dingies. I waited until the third to answer. Didn't want to seem too eager.

"Hello," I said, my voice already hollow, like it was echoing from outside my body. Opioids are magic like that.

"Ms. Kodimer? This is Mike Stern. I'm sorry to tell you that you didn't get the reporter position."

"What?" I croaked, but Mike didn't hear. He'd already hung up. L.A. was the capital of transactional exchanges—no time wasted on niceties when you were disposable. The rage was immediate. I hurled my glass against the yellow-green wallpaper. Purple syrup streaked down the wall in slow rivulets. Then everything went black.

Wine + pills + fury = blackout.

What I don't remember, my brain has since filled in. Bloated with Harvey's, numbed with pills, heavy with disappointment, I staggered out of my apartment, keys in hand, on autopilot. My body knew the route: behind the wheel, pointed toward the Westwood Ho Market. I needed more—always more—to cauterize the pain.

Accounts vary, but I raised enough hell in the supermarket that the manager threatened to call the cops. "Leave!" He was, in point of fact, screaming. Miracle of miracles—I listened. Probably because I knew orange jumpsuit wasn't my color. Not with auburn hair.

I drove off in my yellow Oldsmobile.

Two blocks later, I sideswiped a parked car. Being the "responsible" drunk I was, I pulled over, stumbled up to the house, and confessed. The homeowner jotted down my license number and insurance info, thanked me for my honesty. That compliment carried me back to my car glowing—though it was just the Harvey's talking.

Unfortunately, the Oldsmobile still ran. Five minutes later, I plowed into another parked car.

This time there was no award for honesty. My blood alcohol was sky-high, pills uncountable. I didn't even feel it when my face slammed into the steering wheel—eight teeth gone, blood everywhere, concussion to boot. My dog bolted from the back seat, smart enough to flee the wreckage that was our lives, distilled and captured in that instant.

I left the car, stumbled home, and collapsed into a blackout sleep.

When I woke, I tasted blood and emptiness where my front teeth had been. The dog was missing. Memories came in pieces: crashes, blood, headlights.

And what did I do next? What does any seasoned addict do after smashing into two parked cars?

I went to the hospital for *more* drugs.

It never occurred to me that I had an alcohol or drug problem. Not when I could have—should have—gone to jail. Not even later, when I found my dog safe at the pound, and spun the story to the volunteer who reluctantly handed him back.

And no—this wasn't rock bottom.

I carried on like that for three more years, chasing numbness, until one day a little voice inside me whispered: *I've had enough.*

No fireworks, no drama. Just surrender.

I got sober. I stayed sober—for thirty years.

Like most good things as advertised, it didn't last.

13. RECOVERY ROUND ONE

Everyone knows a cat has nine lives. I've had fewer—so far—but it begs the question, since we're talking about addiction (and we are): How many recoveries do I have left?

My first recovery, like my first love, is worth recounting.

It was 1983. I was 38 and addicted to Valium. I was also drinking—not all day, not yet—but enough. I managed to stop drinking for a while, but I couldn't let go of my little yellow buddies. They gave me just enough courage to do absolutely nothing with my life.

It didn't take too many interminable, foggy stretches of lethargy to realize that what I thought was helping me was destroying both my body and my will. I asked my psychiatrist at the time—a savior-turned-drug-dealer in a suit and tie in Century City—if he could help me get off Valium. He assured me, with all the empathy of a fern, that he could not.

One stormy day in May, I stomped out of his office on Wilshire Boulevard, clutching his handwritten prescription like a lifeline. The parking lot was a lake. Water was up to my knees, but I was more worried about the ink smudging on the prescription than about getting electrocuted. God forbid the script become unreadable and therefore unfillable. Everything was wrong with this picture. But I was far too deep in denial to notice I had a problem.

Then came a fluke, or fate.

A writing instructor I knew mentioned Overeaters Anonymous—OA—after casually telling me I'd be prettier if I lost some weight. That one-two punch sent me to my first OA meeting. A dozen women and one shell-shocked man sat in a circle, chanting the mantra of abstinence.

Abstinence? What even was that? I understood self-abnegation. But this was different. This was confusing. I was about to flee when I overheard someone say they were heading to another 12-step meeting: Alcoholics Anonymous.

Since I was doing absolutely nothing productive that year, I figured: *Why not*?

The clubhouse was on Ohio Street in West L.A. There must have been over a hundred people in that room, poised to bear their souls. I wanted to turn and run but instead sat stock still in my chair. Fear took a back seat when the first speaker told *my* story. She was addicted to pills—so was I. She had no off-switch—same. For the first time, I felt at home.

The meeting ended with tears, hugs, and something resembling hope. I was making my way toward the exit when a woman with kind eyes approached me.

"Are you an alcoholic?" she asked gently.

"No," I blurted. Not considering that blacking out and hitting two parked cars in the vehicle my parents bought me might qualify me as one.

She waited, just long enough for the truth to bubble up.

"I'm addicted to pills," I added, almost whispering. "Mostly Valium."

"So was I," she said. "That was ten years ago. I haven't had a pill since."

That had to be a miracle. And I was in the market for miracles.

Her name was Sharon. She gave me her phone number and told me to call. Naturally, I assumed she wanted something—money, probably. But when I called the next day, she asked for nothing. She just wanted to help.

And that, to me, *was* the miracle.

She told me I couldn't do this alone. I needed help. She suggested I go to a renowned chemical dependency center nearby. Problem was, I had no money. But my parents did. Oodles of it. Surely, they'd help. Wouldn't they?

I hadn't spoken to them in years.

But in an uncharacteristic moment of naked honesty, I called my mother and told her everything. She, in turn, called my father. And that same day, I entered treatment.

I took my last pill—my last one for the next 30 years—*that* day.

Until I relapsed.

I've since learned that relapse is part of recovery. And my first was as spectacular as it was tragic.

14. THE APARTMENT GIRL FOR WHOM THE EARTH MOVED

In 1994, I was an apartment gal in Southern California. More Valley than Hollywood, but close enough to inhale the ethos of ambition and self-improvement. That was the year a 6.7 magnitude Northridge earthquake—an act of God (as I like to call Her)—shook me out of my two-bedroom apartment and into a townhouse. At the time, the idea of owning a home felt impossible. I was a long-established apartment gal. I took baby steps. Toddler-sized, really. Half-steps, tottering, never bold.

My mother trained me to view full steps as indulgent. Apartment gals don't indulge. We nibble at life. We sip. We don't dive. We edge.

Against all odds, I eventually went from a dank, drug-infested one-bedroom flat to a cheerful one-bedroom flat with extremely rude neighbors who believed three a.m. was concert o'clock. Not that they were musicians. Just inconsiderate people with questionable taste in music. There's only so much R.E.M. one can endure in the wee hours. That led me to a two-bedroom apartment—a big move for me. Safe. Solid. Until the earth moved under my feet and catapulted me into a townhouse. Earthquakes have a way of creating momentum.

One day I woke up in a home with cathedral ceilings and marble floors. I was as shocked as my mother—especially since I could still hear her shouting in my head:

Think small.
Live small.
Be tiny.

Eventually, I stuck the landing. I found myself in a 2,300 square-foot house on the ocean. A fortress. The apartment gal had broken the mold.

The downside was that my apartment-gal mentality came with me. The space was grand. My thinking was not. My aspirational habits were still forming but my fears were still governing.

Not surprisingly, I ended up back in an SLE. One step forward, twelve steps back—back to small rooms, shared kitchens and frayed nerves.

And that, truly, is where the real journey began.

15. MY SAUCY SURROGATE MOTHER

I was shy, scared, and forty when I walked into my first AA meeting in search of a safety net. Suffice it to say I did *not* jump in with both feet. Everything frightened me—people, bugs, Arby's hamburgers.

Yet I persisted through that first year, chewing the scenery by design. I strategically snuck in late and slipped out early. People came to know that the corner chair in the last row was mine. I understood the assignment—show up, stay sober, earn karmic points for participation. I kept my stone-like detachment though. I never shared. Not my experiences, not my emotions. Not surprisingly, no one threw me that net.

And yet … change came for me anyway, the way it comes for everyone who sticks around long enough.

Her name was Willa. She made eye contact while I was studiously avoiding it. She even leaned in—subtly but intentionally—to show she was listening. Her spidey-sense registered how frightened and lonely I was.

"Hi," she said. "Any interest in blowing this pop stand for a small, women-only meeting at my friend's apartment in West Hollywood?"

Sounds uncomfortable, I thought.

"Sure," I said.

We drove together the following Wednesday. And every Wednesday after that, for ten years.

The elderly woman who whipped open the door was elegant—and in this way only—reminiscent of my mother.

The moment felt formal. My spine straightened involuntarily. My upper lip quivered. I resisted the urge to salute her.

"I am Elena," she said, her piercing blue eyes framed by majestic waves of silver hair. She was *very* put together.

"Char," I murmured.

When she hugged me hello, my exoskeleton evaporated. I would've followed her anywhere.

Her apartment was nondescript. The people inside were *not*.

Wednesdays became a ritual. A new addiction. I held on for dear life.

Elena embraced me—physically, emotionally, spiritually—in a way a certain mother of mine never had. I *craved* Wednesday nights, for the wisdom, yes, but also for the hugs. I became a first-rate hugger thanks to her.

Periodically, she would send me actual letters (handwritten—on stationery) telling me how much she loved me. I remember ripping one open and thinking, *Oh! This is how people love.*

One of my favorite memories of Elena has nothing to do with hugs. It has to do with condiments. Despite her class and elegance, Elena was no *gourmand.* Before each Wednesday meeting, we'd eat at a nearby restaurant—and she would drench her food in sauces. No exceptions. She loved her condiments with religious fervor.

When she died, I stopped eating sauce. All of it. Cold turkey. I didn't want the stabbing reminder of her absence in every squirt of Sriracha.

Hindsight gives you a new lens.

Elena wasn't just a friend. She was my surrogate mother. She gifted me two things I never got from my family of origin: belonging and a voice.

In my first family, I was the little girl with the big bow who didn't know how to open her mouth—because no one ever encouraged her to do so. In my chosen family, I could say it out loud, say it clearly, say it with conviction—and still be loved.

I have Willa to thank for introducing me to Elena. And Elena to thank for teaching me that I am worthy of hugs, of love, of redemption.

And maybe even a little extra sauce.

16. THIRD-STEP PRAYER

In AA, we learn the Third Step Prayer:

God, I offer myself to Thee—to build with me and do with me as Thou wilt. Relieve me of the bondage of self, that I may better do Thy will. Take away my difficulties, that victory over them may bear witness to those I would help of Thy power, Thy love, and Thy way of life. May I do Thy will always.

The corresponding Third Step reads:

Made a decision to turn our will and our lives over to the care of God as we understood Him.

The step—and the prayer—are invitations. To gratitude. To humility. To surrender. And, for me, to just a dash of panic. It also sparks a familiar, circular dialogue with my Higher Power—whom I call "HP" to keep things casual. I do love a little deflection through humor.

The internal loop often goes something like this:

HP: So ... you want to be a stand-up comedian now?

Me: Yes! But I'm terrified. Help, help, help. Little Char is flailing. SOS.

HP: Then stop flailing. Face the music. Aren't you tired of living inauthentically?

Me: I just want a nibble out of life. I won't hurt anyone but myself. I pinky swear.

HP: Then it's settled. Get out of your own way. Step through the gate. Release. Unleash. Also ... get a dog.

In 2021, mid-pandemic and mid-reckoning, I followed the last part of that divine directive. I got myself a Cavalier King Charles Spaniel—a royal breed for a recovering Jewish princess. He was eight months old and offensively expensive. Still, he was a bargain.

I named him Lucky. But the truth? I was the lucky one.

Some days, I wonder if *he* thinks he drew the short straw. I can't be easy. My moods swing like wrecking balls. And yet—when I'm spiraling, he stays right next to me. On my lap in the car. Under the table at meals. Underfoot, on purpose. He leans in. Always.

It's as if he knows. And he doesn't ask why.

He's a dog. I don't need to understand. I only need to receive his love.

17. SMOOTH SAILING BACK TO SELF

One of my several stays in an SLE was in the exclusive town of Tiburon, California. I had my own private room overlooking the bay—and I was sober. I was finally free. Or so I thought.

I ventured out to an AA meeting one night and ran into a guy from my Harbor Hill cohort. We were having a pleasant evening until he turned to me and said, "If anyone relapses, it'll be you."

I was devastated.

Unmoored and pissed off, I stamped that confrontational message onto my heart and carried it back to my room. The minute I was alone, I took a half bottle of pills and blacked out.

I'd show him.

Revenge-using? To hurt only myself? No problem.

Proving him right became my latest—and lowest—achievement.

In the morning, I was taken to the local hospital, with which I would soon become very familiar. When I woke up, I was strapped to a gurney, gazing up into the eyes of an RN.

"You're okay, honey. You're on suicide watch."

What? I thought, but my voice didn't work. I wanted to tell her I was frightened, not crazy. I wanted out of the restraints.

Then it occurred to me, as I was strapped down and supine.

Maybe I was some kind of crazy. The professionals seemed to think so. That's why I was bound like a convict.

Another nurse approached with a blood pressure cuff. I turned my head to read the meter: 200/200.

"You're at high risk for a stroke. I want you to breathe deeply with me," she said.

I tried, but all I could picture was a carnival barker yelling: *Step right up, ladies and gentlemen! This woman may stroke out or off herself—don't miss the show!*

I lived through that part. But it felt like I was floating above it all, watching someone else live it.

Disassociation, my therapists would later call it. A coping mechanism.

My sense of hearing, at least, was intact. People were speaking about me in the third person, as if I weren't there. My life—prostrate and restrained—was in their hands.

"Should we send her to ICU or psych?"

Neither! I wanted to scream. But like in a dream, no words came.

While they debated my fate, a case manager appeared beside the gurney. She launched into a barrage of questions designed to determine whether I was, in fact, a danger to myself.

"Nope, I'm good," I said loud and clear, surprising myself. (Apparently, the naloxone injection, IV drip, and assisted ventilation had kicked in.)

I tried to sell her my story: I'd recently rounded a corner, two months clean after a three-year opioid spiral.

"This was just a little setback," I explained. "Triggered by a flippant, thoughtless friend. But suicidal? Me? Never."

She wasn't buying it.

After signing some official-looking forms, she barked out to the weekend crew: "To the psych ward."

Away. Take her away. She didn't bother looking back to meet my desperate gaze.

"Please," I begged. "I don't have any track marks. I'm just an ordinary pill-popper."

And if you've got more, I'm happy to take them.

Two large men spun the gurney 180 degrees with impressive efficiency.

Smooth sailing down the corridor.

They were well trained. They didn't make eye contact.

Tears slid down my temples and into my hair when I heard:

"KODIMER! YOU CAN GO HOME NOW!"

To this day, I don't know what happened.

Maybe the nurse was trying to scare me straight. Maybe a doctor glanced at my chart and decided I didn't meet 5150 criteria (or as we say in California, short-term crazy).

I came in that night assessed as a suicidal maniac.

I walked out a run-of-the-mill drug addict.

Free—but alone.

Again.

18. DAVE AND JACK, MY BODYGUARDS

After being discharged from the ER, I joined the ranks of the lost, the abandoned, the unhoused. My fall from promising was nothing if not definitive.

I called the manager of the SLE from the ER. She was unequivocal: I was not welcome to return. The lawyers had weighed in. I was now a liability—especially if I showed up alone. I would need sober companions, around the clock.

My next call was to an AA friend, who sprang into action. Within the hour, Dave and Jack—two guys from AA central casting—pulled into the tree-lined circular drive of the toney hospital. They knew I was their gal: pallid, empty handed, sleep deprived. Turns out, drug-induced unconsciousness doesn't replenish the soul.

The risk of missteps, especially for suicidal addicts, is high in the first 30 days after relapse. I was no exception. Dave and Jack would be my sober bodyguards for the month. I would be monitored 24/7—except, mercifully, for solo bathroom breaks, during which one of them would stand guard outside the door.

You'd think having zero alone time would feel suffocating.

Au contraire! I never had so much fun. Also—bodyguards! I didn't get this kind of attention in L.A., or, frankly, ever. We went sightseeing, cruised through the countryside, and ate our way across Marin County.

I had forgotten fun. They reminded me.

Dave was an ex-con who'd gotten sober and wanted to help others—especially himself. *How much money can I make off these drunken slobs?* was his motto. I adored his candor. He'd committed the infamous 13th step of AA by getting someone pregnant. Never married her. Always thinking of himself first. I respected the consistency.

Jack, on the other hand, was a lover of food. Morning, noon, and night—he never met a calorie he didn't like. He must've weighed 500 pounds. I later tried to introduce him to Overeaters Anonymous, but he wanted no part of it. "Food is my medicine," he said. I couldn't argue.

Dave, the felon, turned out to be the softer of the two. He was a silent supporter, a steady shadow, and someone for whom I'll always be grateful.

When my time at the SLE—including my fortnight with Dave and Jack—came to an end (read: I needed a "higher level of care"), it was off to rehab again. This time: Petaluma, California. "The egg basket of the world," where not just chickens but pigs, cows, and horses reside. And those animals, I must say, were far cleaner than my co-residents.

After five months, just before discharge, I was informed of a suspicious lump in my breast. I went in for a biopsy and waited. The nurse shared the results over speakerphone in the car as Dave and Jack drove me to

Petaluma: "Negative." They clapped and cheered while I exhaled.

I'd been given yet another pass in life. My contract was extended.

A blessed break … until the doors of that next rehab swung open, and I walked through the looking glass again.

19. TO REHAB WE GO AGAIN AND AGAIN

When I limped through the doors to Harbor Hill Rehabilitation Center, I knew immediately: this was not my scene. The residents were younger—much younger. Hygiene standards were ... optional. Showers seemed elusive. Flushing, rare. Cleaning hair out of the drain? Apparently unheard of.

I'm not a neat freak, but rehab sure pushed me in that direction.

This was, after all, Northern California, otherwise known as the place where privileged white people go to flex, procreate, and cultivate ostensibly perfect selves and families. It's a county infused with the promise that you'll never have to do anything for your actual, capital-S Self—because someone else (usually paid help, occasionally a relative) has already handled it. Thank you, next.

So, it was much to my surprise—shock, really—to learn upon arrival at my first stint in rehab here that room service was not a thing.

What do you mean there's no room service? Where are we? Don't you know who I am? I kept these questions to myself.

I missed my maid. There, I said it. If only Rocio was with me, everything would have been alright. As an elder, surely, I deserved a perk now and then. I made an appointment with the director.

"Thanks for taking the time," I began carefully. "While I appreciate everything you're doing here, I'm afraid I might not be ... suitable. I'm a bit high maintenance without my support system."

"There's always an adjustment period," she said. "How about I schedule a meeting with your care-team therapist tomorrow to discuss your concerns?"

I agreed, though I remained deeply dubious.

To my surprise, the therapist was gentle, smart, and—hallelujah—competent. A winner in a long line of losers. I wanted to please him. So, I stayed.

That meeting never happened.

By the end of a grueling ten weeks, however, my blood pressure had soared to 200/135. I was repeatedly carted off to the ER, where one particularly charmless doctor told me I was experiencing "garden-variety anxiety" and asked me not to come back.

I relayed all this to my kind therapist, who agreed it was time for me to go. But—under no circumstances—was I to return to Los Angeles. He had a better idea.

Enter *Together We Can*, a sober living environment with possibilities. I arrived with a plan: I would not make my bed, fold my clothes, or vacuum. A committee convened.

This was a long time ago, so a few hours later—having unpacked my one bag into my 10 x 12 cell—I paged with purpose through a thick yellow phone book marked in Sharpie: DO NOT REMOVE. Under "Maid Service," the only listing was Merry Maids. This would not do.

The next day, I presented my talking points to the flat-affect committee. I explained Rocio's essential role in my life and offered to pay double. They made an exception.

I called Rocio that night from our shared phone.

"Hi Rocio, it's me—Char. I've relocated to a place in Marin that doesn't offer amenities. Any chance you'd want to relocate for a few months? All expenses paid."

She didn't miss a beat. "Of course, Miss Char."

Problem solved. She arrived the next day. One room for Rocio, one room for me. Two peas in an institutional pod.

Naturally, my next line of inquiry was whether the exorbitantly priced program included valet services or car rentals. Reasonable questions, if you ask me. But the intake coordinator did not indulge me. She simply stared.

Nyet, nyet, and nyet, said her eyes.

Helga (not her real name, but it fits) eventually turned out to be a surprising ray of sunshine at what I came to regard as a *de facto* prison. I somehow survived eight weeks of group sessions, group meals, group circles, group activities, and group reflections. Removed from humanity but immersed with fellow inmates who shared only one thing with me: addiction.

After three months of close quarters, I itched to escape. I moved into a house on the water, complete with adorable quacking ducks. A mini mansion, by my standards. The "Apartment Gal" had finally graduated to a home.

Six months earlier, I'd checked into rehab.

Now I had space. Freedom. Ducks.

But could I handle it? A real home? Would it swallow me up? Did I deserve it? Would I swerve into the background again, rendering myself invisible, like I had so many times before?

The answers soon became self-evident.

20. PRESCRIPTION FOR A LIFE LESS LIVED

2017 Reflections

I am a strong, powerful woman with a small potato who aspires to be a large yam.

I remind myself of that because—in a land not so far away (SoCal), in another life—I was a small, weak woman with *no* potato. (Potato being a metaphor for life, if you're playing along at home.)

Here's how my unraveling went:

1. I was ill—physically and mentally—and was prescribed an antipsychotic drug.

2. Over time, that drug stopped working.

3. I became ill again—scary-ill, Thorazine-ill, padded-room ill.

4. My classes became overwhelming.

5. I quit my internship.

6. I was diagnosed with fibromyalgia, so I followed the diagnosis—barely leaving the couch, always exhausted. The couch and I became symbiotic. We existed, together, for years.

7. My doctor prescribed codeine for my pain.

8. As an addict (with years of sobriety under my belt), I could not have been happier.

9. I was relieved, albeit temporarily, from my chronically miserable life—courtesy of Big Pharma and Dr. Enabler.

10. But even in that haze, I recognized it: This was not salvation. This was a reprieve—and a slow grave, a beginning of the end. A living death.

And yet—I would be revived to see another day.

21. ALL-AMERICAN VICTIM

Before I became a strong powerful woman with a small potato, I was the All-American Victim. I was afraid to live. Instead, I lived small, modeling my tiny mother, which is to say I barely lived.

For most of my life, I have been in a prison of my own making. I never got married, never had children and never had a career. I didn't step out of the box. Too scary. It was always safe in my prison.

Anytime I tried to get out of prison, I landed in pain. For as long as I can remember, I've awakened to pain, endured pain throughout each day and went to bed in pain.

Naturally, I did not leave my carefully constructed cell.

I knew no other way to live or love.

It's understood that we hold the key to our prison. I am no exception. After years of serial ailments, from fibromyalgia to back surgery, my *modus operandi* was to put myself in enough pain to get the key to kingdom: my meds. My key was my medicine, and I knew how to get it.

So strong was my ability to *create my world of pain* that I once made it so severe that I could not walk. My pain led to my wheelchair which led to my back surgery which again led to the key to the kingdom: my meds. Full circle, courtesy of me!

The surgery had no chance of succeeding because I was dead set on probing for pain. I was powerful *and* helpless, which is harder than it looks.

I was not comfortable taking small steps, much less big leaps. Steps and leaps came with anxiety and panic. I woke up each morning and greeted the day. *Hello Day!* And that is when the panic grabbed me by the neck. Steps and leaps and panic attacks, I learned, came with more meds.

Moving into a new house, for example, induced panic and fear. Once frightened, I put myself in pain. Freeze or retreat; those were my options, always with medication, holding me "together."

On August 18, 2017, after 72 years in my Charlene-edition prison, I finally dropped the rock and caught the rope. (As will be explained.) A new beginning. A miracle. I've experienced several true miracles since I've been sober.

I had been a bit of an Alcoholics Anonymous ("AA") skeptic, but who was I to deny that there is something—some "higher power" or "hp" as we say—taking care of us?

I woke up that morning in acute pain, per usual. I sat on my bed, clammy, limbs aching, wanting to die.

Instead, I got my ass out of bed and went to a meeting.

I did not say a word in that meeting. I sat there, sweat beading above my eyes. And yet I stuck it out. Instead of complaining about my pain, I asked how I could be of service.

As soon as I did—and this is the bit with the miracle—my pain dissolved.

I realize now that I wasn't alone in that chair. With me—within me—was my inner child. I didn't banish her that day. I invited her in. I gave her permission to be there and permission to live, pain-free.

After 72 years, mini-Char finally had a mommy who would take care of her. Listen to her. Hug her. She had, for what felt like the first time, a mother who would protect her and hold her hand as she stepped out into the world.

The little girl was scared. What if she reverted to her old ways? This was new territory for her. She would need help. Lots of help. No one expected her to do this perfectly. Mistakes would be made; she was sure of it. Yet, the little girl embarked on her new life, this time with a mother who assured her she would be there every step of the way.

Thankfully, the little girl didn't forget to pack her Band-Aids for the journey.

22. HANDLE WITH CARE — AND OTHER RE-MOTHERING TIPS

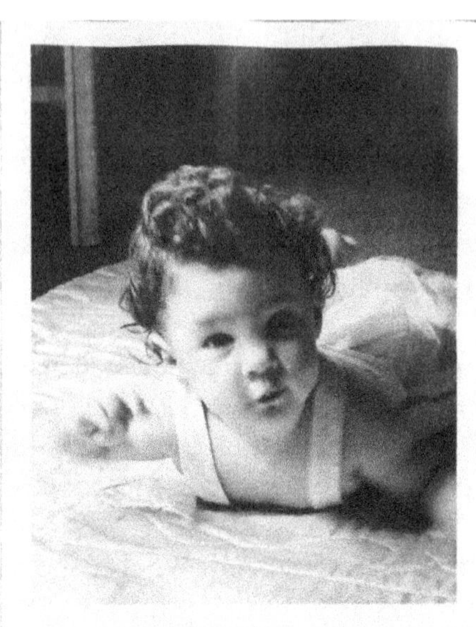

August 25, 2017

Having recently spent time with my inner child, I'm here to report she's not always good company.

Fear is her only gear. When she gets scared, she taps into her pain so she can either (1) do nothing or (2) get drugs. Her role, in her family of origin, was Victim. Conscripted Victim, to be more accurate. She was consigned to complaining, yearning, and being uncomfortable—always. She wasn't the only one, but the others masked their neuroses and mental illness like champs.

When I pull focus to my 72-year-old Self, I'm less inclined to wallow in misery or fear. I'm more inclined to see that little girl as vulnerable. I grant her dispensation. She was a *child,* for f#ck's sake. Her mother never held her—or even her hand—because she was too busy looking in the mirror.

Does that ruin a child? No.

But it doesn't help.

Neither did being sent to pick up my father's tranquilizers as a teenager. If they worked for him, why wouldn't they work for young Char Char? Who could blame me for modeling what I saw: that pain could be blunted—and maybe even avoided—through pills.

Now I regard the younger me as a sentient, imperfect being who simply wanted to be held, loved, and supported. And I believe what my therapist tells me: *It's not too late to re-mother yourself.*

So that's what I'll do.

I'll throw my inner child a buoy. She'll take it, knowing she never again has to be afraid or alone.

And when pain and fear rear their familiar heads, I'll remind her she has choices:

She can choose adventure over nightmare.
New over known.
Excitement over fear.

Making mistakes—and learning from them—over staying small, hidden, cowering.

In a word: Living.

23. FROM IDENTIFIABLE PATIENT TO GOOD MOTHER

August 2017

Every family has an Identifiable Patient—the "IP." I didn't *choose* the role of victim, but I sure inhabited it. Fully. For a long, long time.

When I was scared—and I was scared often—that fear either *became* pain or I manufactured it. Pain was my way in. It was my only strategy. It was how I coped.

Thankfully, my role as the alone, unsafe IP was time limited.

According to Internal Family Systems therapy (IFS), also known as "parts work," every person has a Self—that essential core that is calm, compassionate, curious, creative, and whole. Alongside the Self, we have "subpersonalities": managers, firefighters, protectors. Each with a job. Each trying to help.

But those subpersonalities can hijack us. They spring into action to protect our wounded parts—the "exiles." The parts we pushed underground long ago.

IFS taught me that my own exile—the IP—was also my inner child. She was born the moment I was repeatedly shamed, rejected, and criticized by the people who were supposed to love me most. It's no wonder my protector part reached for pills. Distraction and numbness were easier than confronting grief, sadness, or the ache of being unwanted.

But addiction kept me stuck. Numbing out meant never healing. How could my inner child thrive if no one ever took care of her? Little Char disappeared. She went underground the day I started using.

But recently … she popped up.

She was feisty. Fiery. Carefree. She wanted to dance. I'd been waiting for her my whole life.

I knew it was time. I had to take care of her.

That meant becoming someone I'd never had: The Good Mother.

At first, I wasn't sure I could do it. My Good Mother part was new, unsure, wobbly. But she knew job one: listen.

Little Char spoke clearly. She was in pain. She'd used pain to get attention from a mother too busy applying makeup or cleaning out drawers to make time for her. My Good Mother heard that truth without flinching. She didn't judge it. She just held it.

Then came job two: comfort**.** I ordered myself a blankie. An adult blankie. Cashmere, because why not? If I was going to re-parent, I was going to do it right. Little Char never had a blankie. She deserved this one.

Job three: feel the feelings.

Anger came first. Righteous, volcanic anger followed. Little Char had been sold out, neglected, stifled. Left behind.

I had long channeled my anger through skin picking—furious and unrelenting. Is that what happens to under-loved kids? They grow up enraged and stuck, demanding a battalion of caretakers to make up for what their families never gave them?

Maybe.

But even if my family never cared, my Good Mother did.

And she reminded me: I could still recover what's left. I could still build what's ahead. *For Little Char's sake.*

Recreating my family of origin—this time with love and care—is the essential work of my life. Marin gave me a fresh start, a new house, and enough quiet to hear my Good Mother's voice.

She is here now.

She will re-parent Little Char.

She will dance with her.

Little Char, for her part, is not to blame. She is sweet. She is adorable. And she *loves* to dance.

To paraphrase Gene Kelly:

She will dance, love, joy, and dream.

And my Good Mother will bear witness.

And nurture her re-birth.

24. FILLING THE HOLE IN THE SOUL

September 22, 2017

I am 72 years old, and I can't wait to live.

I'm excited about life. This is novel!

I feel undeserving, which is hard to admit. I've never known how to enjoy life because I was stuck—physically, emotionally. But now that I'm healing, thanks to my higher power and support team, I'm allowing myself this moment of contentment. Surveying the scene. Feeling sated.

This is finally *my* life, curated by *me*.

Suffice it to say, it took a while.

It feels grand—my brand of grand—the kind that fills the empty hole inside. The kind money can't buy.

That empty hole is starting to fill up—not with candy, doughnuts, or jewelry—but with something beautiful. Something I've been searching for my whole life.

It's called gratitude.

The ticket, I think, is simply to look around and *notice*—the people, the positive, the goodness. And to receive it. To let it in.

Because we're worthy of being loved.

Each one of us.

25. HOLIDAYS ON ICE

December 2019

Female friends come into my life—and then they leave. When they do, it feels like a breakup.

Take Gabby, for example.

I was genuinely excited to go wedding dress shopping with her. Her big day was just around the corner (eleven months later, but still). Time was of the essence, or so I thought. But she kept canceling our plans.

"Sick."

"Tired."

"Double-booked."

I finally got the message.

I vented to others, replayed it in my mind, couldn't let it go. I texted her: *What is going on with us?*

She replied the next day. Her words cut straight to the core: *We are just not as close as we used to be.*

True.

Obvious.

Undeniable.

Still felt like a punch in the gut.

I took it for what it was: rejection, plain and simple.

Over time, Gabby-adjacent friends began subtly pulling away too—especially at her raucous bingo parties. I was already a square peg in a round hole at those gatherings. But I went anyway. I wanted connection. Community. Friends.

When Gabby dusted me, it felt like a divorce. And it became clear her friends were choosing sides. Team Gabby, of course. Why wouldn't they be? She sings opera, has a big, magnetic personality and throws loud parties with prizes.

And me?

I'm itty-bitty, imperceptible Char Char, stuffed with feelings. Feelings like jealousy. Feelings that have nowhere to go and just sit there, gnawing at my insides. Feelings that sap my energy and whisper, *you are not enough.*

The addict-obsessive in me wants to fix it. Patch it. Make it right. Wants to crawl back into Gabby's orbit, be back in her league.

But the recovering addict-obsessive in me—the wiser part—knows this: I need to be around people who love the highly imperfect me.

Easier said than done. Especially during the holidays, when those people seem few and far between.

Ho, ho, home alone—unless you count my cat, Bruno.

Bruno appears bored with all aspects of his life, including his owner.

Still, I'll take his apathy over Gabby's rejection any day of the week.

26. ON THE TOPIC OF BUILDING THE WALL

2019

Here are a couple fun facts about aging as a woman:

Your vaginal walls will thin.

You will lose your hearing and your eyesight—likely at the same time—so that when you're tasked with inserting a pill into your vagina (to "strengthen the wall," courtesy of dwindling estrogen), you can't see what you're doing.

This may very well be the closest you've come to masturbating in years.

As easy as it sounds, there's a 60 percent chance that pill will fall to the floor when you stand up. You will—sacrificing your last shred of dignity—wash it off and insert it again.

When it finally stays in on the third try, at age 75, this will be your biggest victory of the weekend.

And you'll be a little smug about it.

Because you'll take your wins—however small, however slippery.

Tomorrow will bring another round of forgetting: *Did I brush my teeth? Take my insulin? Count my pills?*

You'll lean into acceptance, armed with the world-weary knowledge that the so-called "Golden Years" are a tarnished tragicomedy.

And you'll be okay with that.

Because you'll keep soldiering on, into the indistinct, uncomfortable unknown.

27. HIT ME WITH YOUR BEST SPOT

2019

My night sweats, once chalked up to menopause, have taken on a new, mysterious origin and an unbearable persistence. I'm supposed to be *past* this particular indignity. In fact, at 75, I'm supposed to be past *just about everything.*

But the new normal is there's no getting past anything. Everything shifts—underfoot, overhead—and not for the better.

Case in point: my freckles. Once charming, they turned into age spots *overnight*. No warning. No vote. Just, boom—welcome to the next phase of "What fresh hell is this?"

The apotheosis—the precise moment I crossed the Rubicon from "older" to "just plain old"—took place in the humble confines of a nail salon. I was getting a pedicure. My technician, Lan, rolled up my pant leg and revealed a shrunken limb—no longer the supple calf of yesteryear, but a veiny, crepey sheath draped over bone and doubt.

Dead center, equidistant between knee and ankle, was a bold, coppery DOT.

I scrubbed at it with alarm. It didn't budge.

Lan shrieked with glee: "Ah, *age spot!*"

As if we'd hit bingo.

Turns out, that lone dot was just the scout for a full-blown invasion—a constellation of what a prepubescent physician's assistant would later call "starburst sunspots." Euphemisms abound when toddlers in lab coats talk to the elderly.

She examined me with a headlamp and magnifying glass like I was an artifact.

But—hope lives! —she had a salve. A miracle cream. It would "reverse aging," she promised, like we were talking about a return policy.

Sure, it was expensive. But what price would you pay to have the dewy, porcelain skin of a newborn? She slathered it all over me, liberally, to zap the spots into oblivion. It stung. I welcomed the burn.

Four appointments later, the only thing that had disappeared was the green stuff from my wallet. "Stubborn," she said, with a helpless shrug. "No guarantees."

Of course not. I should've read the fine print—only I *couldn't*, thanks to my cataracts and severe astigmatism.

Just as I was contemplating a pricier miracle, something new arrived: bruises.

Red, purple, blue. If I bumped the kitchen counter, a hematoma the size of Texas bloomed on my hip. If I fished a tissue from my purse, my hand came out looking like a Jackson Pollock painting.

Eventually, all of it—spots, bruises, broken capillaries, failing vision—became *less surprising than expected*. That's when I knew: the quest for agelessness was lost.

But surrender? No. Not quite.

Instead, I raise my gnarled, freckled, spotted hand to the sky and say: *Go ahead. Hit me with your best spot.*

28. EVERYBODY NEEDS A SLEEP BUDDY

This is the story of a woman who spent seven-plus decades not being who she wanted to be. And then, just as she became her true self—engaged, creative, funny, a do-gooder—she got Parkinson's.

Put differently: the day I finally helped myself to the large potato—the yam that symbolized My Best Life—my finger started to tremble. My gait wobbled. All signs pointed to Parkinson's.

Excerpts from my journal, lightly edited:

Sept. 5, 2021: What (and Who) I Have Become

I have Parkinson's. I'm a mess. A mess with resources.

I have staff. Thank God for my inheritance, or I'd be long gone.

My MVP is Wendall, my wonderful assistant.

Then there's Lexie, my human sleep-aid. Yes, I need someone to hunker down with me to sleep.

There's also Ivy, my part-time trainer—"part-time" because she doesn't always show up. But I love her, so I give her a pass. Wendall, understandably, gets weary. I thus hired an assistant for my assistant. Enter tobacco-chewing Jake, who scrubs the tile with a toothbrush. Bless him. (Though I sometimes wonder if I should fire Jake just to keep Wendall from getting jealous. You see the dilemma.)

It's like *The Brady Bunch for the Elderly*. Maybe I should take them on the road. Call it *Char Char's Coterie*

Sept. 6, 2021: Becoming My Father

Didn't sleep. Why would I? Had an energy drink. Regret.

Tremor in my index finger makes writing hard. All signs—but not my finger, because it can't point—say Parkinson's.

It's one of the worst illnesses, so of course I have it.

I'll talk to Dr. Good, my GP. She referred me to a neurologist. First available appointment? January. Months away. Goodbye, holidays.

My father had Parkinson's (thanks, Dad!), but diabetes killed him. Slowly.

Even when he couldn't walk or sleep or eat, I was still afraid of him.

He'd eat a popsicle, blue-dye goo dripping down his chin, with his beloved talk radio buzzing in the background, smiling. The simplest things made him smile. Childlike.

Then his time was up.

When will mine be up?

I'm shrinking. I used to be 5'3". Now I'm 5'0". Soon I'll be circus ready. I'll start *Char Char's Circus for the Shrunken and Slightly Mad.*

But no fire. FAA rules.

Yes, I'm in a cult of sorts: Food Addicts Anonymous. It's the only thing that curbs my grazing. I'm not a cow, but I graze like one. I'm becoming my mother *and* my father. There's a musical in here somewhere.

So far, we have a TV show, a circus, and a musical. The spin-offs are endless. Everyone is aging. Relatable content!

I can't stop eating, drinking, drugging, or shopping. But I *can* stop sleeping. I'm a pro insomniac.

I tried it all: meditation, melatonin, gabapentin. Nothing worked. Until Lexie. My human Ambien.

She puts me to bed at 11 p.m., says, "Nighty-night, Char Char, I love you," and that's enough. Until 12:30 a.m. when I wake up thinking about how much I pay her.

I think about firing her. But then I'd be back to square one.

She comes nightly, unless there's a flood—which recently happened. I let her off the hook.

It's all connected. If I don't sleep, I don't lose weight. If I don't dream, I ruminate. If I don't obsess, I panic. And all this while not sleeping.

I obsess about food, shopping (am I wearing the right Johnny Was pajamas to induce sleep?), and now, Parkinson's.

My shopping addiction went dormant when Wendall stopped returning packages. I ran out of under-bed storage.

And yet, Mr. Parkinson's doesn't know who he's dealing with. I'm nothing if not wily and determined.

29. PARKINSON'S, A PRIMER

In 2022, after getting sober—for real this time—I was diagnosed with Parkinson's, an abhorrent, insidious disease. Technically, it's a brain disorder that affects movement, mood, and various systems in the body. "Affects" is a euphemism, of course. A soft word that masks a brutal reality.

Let me vent for a moment. It's important for people to understand the full devastation of this disease—what it does to a person, not just physically, but existentially.

My legs, from toes to knees, feel locked in place. Frozen, rigid, numb—yet somehow painful. Walking is becoming more difficult. I'm afraid of the unhappy ending: a wheelchair, or worse, a bed I never leave. Stiffness is standard when Parkinson's is on the menu.

I don't swallow the way I used to. That's Parkinson's, too. I may eventually lose the ability to swallow altogether—which means I'm already grieving donuts in advance. Add to that chronic constipation, acid reflux, and daily nausea. It's a full house of bodily betrayal.

Sleep? I wish. I have insomnia *every single night*. I wake up at 2 a.m. and pace like a ghost. My body's circadian rhythm is now set to "freakish." During the day, I nod off without warning—sometimes mid-sentence. I feel like a malfunctioning marionette. My social life? It's gone.

I have no idea how I'll feel from one moment to the next. I live in the Twilight Zone. I am preternaturally tired.

Pain is a constant companion. I've seen more specialists than I can count, and none seem to grasp the scale of it. They won't prescribe anything "strong," of course—they're protecting me from myself. But when I'm in the center of the pain cyclone, I want answers.

When will my pain and sleep be acknowledged? Addressed? Ameliorated?

How much more do I have to suffer? Specifically, how much more must I endure *without sleep and in pain*? *When is enough, enough?*

For his final act of stubborn denial, my father chose a feeding tube. That will *not* be my choice.

And yet, there are miracles.

My handwriting has improved. I can still write—an unexpected mitzvah. During my gratitude meditations (which, honestly, have gotten shorter), I try to remember this: I can still share my truth. I can still connect. I can still *mean* something on the page.

I am also surrounded by love.

I will not die alone. And for that, I am deeply grateful.

I won't walk this path alone. I won't forge this awful, aching journey without help. On my worst days, I still have my very Lucky dog, whose snores make me laugh and whose presence keeps me tethered to comfort. If there's a God, Lucky was a divine delivery. So are Wendall, Diana, Hannah, and every soul who shows up for me.

To them, I have something to say:

I could not do this without you.

I love you.

Thank you.

And to Parkinson's, a different kind of message:

Fuck you.

You haven't stopped me yet.

And despite your cruel, debilitating mix of symptoms, I plan to persist.

I've got tools. I've got people. I've endured worse.

I'm a strong woman with a yam—and a life—of my own choosing, thank you very much.

30. ONE THOUSAND (STRESSFUL) NIGHTS

Nightfall, for me, augurs anxiety. Here it comes, people—the nightly struggle to sleep, to finally fucking rest. Tonight, like every night, will be textbook: I will toss and turn like a human rotisserie.

At 9 p.m., my phone pings softly—my nightly reminder to "wind down." Cute. But really, it's just the starting gun at the anxiety racetrack. *There she goes, folks—number seven—off and running at Churchill Downs, racing for a low number. Let's shoot for something dreamy, like 120/80.*

I strap the blood pressure cuff to my arm and breathe in for five … out for five. That should help, right?

I sit still. Sweat trickles from my thinning hair down into my rheumy eyes. My Johnny Was T-shirt clings to my chest. My heart pounds. I feel it behind my eyes. My foot taps—one heart-attacky, two heart-attacky. My pulse reads 108.

Yikes.

The more I obsess about dreadful things, the higher it spikes. It's like my body wants a reason to implode.

When the coroner fills out my death certificate, it'll read: *Cause of death: Anxiety.*

P.S. I want deep red roses on the coffin.

Yes, I am the Queen of Anxiety. It's what I do to myself when life gets too good. Solid friendships? Check. A solid tummy? Check. A whole solid day at 1200 calories? Victory lap.

Held the sugar.
Held the fries.
Held the mayo, the syrup, the gravy.
Hold—hold—HOLD me.

I'm needy even when I'm not asking for anything. You can see it in my eyes, my twitchy body language. When I get needy, I get lonely. When I get lonely, I eat. I know I'm not alone.

Why have one slice of salami when you can have the whole goddamn salami (followed, of course, by nausea, acid reflux, and self-loathing)?

Why do I self-sabotage at every good turn?

These are questions for therapists, philosophers, and my HP.

The answer may be simple: I have no STOP button. I am a bottomless pit. My middle name is MORE.

More, more, and actually—yes please—more. More this. More that. More of all the above.

Even now, as I write this, I can feel the urge swell from somewhere inside me—from the hole in my heart, or my stomach, or my soul.

Unlike Scheherazade, I'm not spinning stories to stay alive. I'm just stuck in a loop, begging for more of the same.

Why?

31. IT'S THREE A.M. AND I'M AFRAID TO DIE

August 19, 2024, 3:00 a.m.: Enough

Today I feel like I've had enough. I'm so weary from being sick.

My mood meme would be: Tired of living but too scared to die.

Dear God,

I know I'm not supposed to ask for myself, but I'd like to string a few good days together. For the past couple of months, I've been nauseous all the time. Sure, it might be a fast way to lose weight and nominally better than Jenny Craig, whose food, to me, tastes like cardboard. And sometimes cardboard with chocolate sauce. And certainly, it's more cost-efficient than Weight Watchers. What's worse is that not only am I nauseous, but I also have acid reflux. I could start my own orchestra with the sounds that come out of me. My friends say I could conduct my own concert. I'm uncomfortable a good deal of the time.

My thoughts naturally yearn for yesteryear when my once strong, beautiful legs propelled me through countless practices on a Masters swim team and held me, unflinching, in down dog. Today, those same legs, from my supple knees down to my cute little toes, are covered with bumps. I don't know what they are nor do the medical professionals.

One doctor I consulted about the mystery bumps and my generalized malaise prefers to diagnose me over Zoom. Let's call her Dr. Zoom, board-certified Dr. Z. She refuses to see me in person. Yay for modern technology. *Something is going to get me, but I can't predict what*, I try to tell her with my anxious expression, squinting at the computer. She can't see me—the whole person I am—through our remote "connection." Telehealth, it's called, although it likely tells her very little about *how I am really doing*.

I turn 80 next year, if I make it. If Dr. Z could meet me in person, we could explore—even co-create—the Octogenarian World I'm about to enter, anticipating and embracing all its inexplicable contradictions. Like why on some days am I determined to push through—to make every day count with the friends I love. And why, on other days, I ask God to let me die in my sleep. My simple cosmic ask is unrealistic, as God would know, since I don't sleep.

I would be bracingly honest with Dr. Z, sharing that I want a quick death. I'd reveal that I'm terrified of losing my memory even as there are hints of it slipping away. I'd state with conviction that I'd rather nod off forever then have hands that shake or legs that can't carry me. *I don't do wheelchairs*, I'd explain (masking fear with my signature mirth), *because they don't make designer wheelchairs*.

She would draw me out, beyond the topics of lumpy legs, relentless insomnia and the expensive comfort dog that snores. I'd reject, again, her suggestion to try the dignity-stripping CPAP machine. My sleep is hard enough as it is without trying to do so with a seemingly suffocating mask-contraption over my face. She would validate me implicitly whilst nodding with soft eyes.

She might even probe for pain in the direction of root causes by asking me about my childhood, to which I'd respond:

I remember the first day of kindergarten like yesterday. I, unironically, had separation anxiety from my mother. She picked me up early from school, brought me home and fed me Oreo cookies. She told me she made them herself. I took the gooey middles out and put them back together in the cookie jar for my brother to find. My only sibling, two years older than me, was the golden child, blond curly hair, bronze skin and a beautiful smile. He could do no wrong. I was jealous so when he wasn't looking, I broke all his toys. He never forgave me. He went on to become a successful neuropsychologist. I went on to have legs covered with bumps and an exercise regimen consisting of making it to the bathroom successfully.

Dr. Z would pretend to empathize, maybe even reach over and put a hand on my shoulder while asking something like: "Did you and your brother mend fences over time?"

Not so much. He got back at me by putting my baby finger in a bike chain, ripping it off my hand and then somehow managing to blame me ... to this day. I think fondly of him each time I look down at my deformed finger. (I would hold it up, dramatic and theatrical, to show her.) *He continued to walk on water until he married an Asian woman and my father disowned him. The fallen, once chosen one, eventually forgave my father for excommunicating him but never forgave me for taking the middle out of the Oreos.*

So, you see, Dr. Z, it hasn't been an easy life and my looming 80s are sure to be just as dreadful as kindergarten. But all is not lost, because my parents, in a spasm of thoughtful preplanning, bought a plot for me in a mausoleum. I'll be next to, but still apart from, my mother for infinity. I wonder if I'll experience separation anxiety when I'm dead.

At this, the doctor, abruptly shifting her gaze back to her computer, would pivot to a new topic: my follow-up appointment by Zoom.

32. CHAR CHAR ON OPIOIDS

Let's talk about opioids.

Who said they hurt people? I'm an opioid addict, and I never hurt anyone.

Well … okay—anyone other than myself.

Sure, I landed in the emergency room five times after overdosing. But I don't necessarily count that as self-harm. It was more like a dangerous version of solitaire—with my usual players: Vicodin, Codeine, and morphine.

Valium was my gateway—my original numbing agent of choice. But when opioids waltzed into the picture, I upgraded. They were more efficient on my path to feeling *absolutely nothing*. I gobbled those pills for years. Somehow, I've been clean now for four decades (save one tiny relapse).

Still, my history follows me wherever I go.

In my mid-to-late 70s, I made frequent trips to the hospital for reasons even the doctors couldn't always explain. Each time, upon entry, the stern triage nurse would ask for my drug history.

"It's complicated—how much time do you have?" I'd quip. You know, to break the ice. Their shifts are long, but mine are longer.

The slogan "once a drug addict, always a drug addict" is sadly true. I know it in my bones.

When people find out you're a former addict or alcoholic, they slap on assumptions like price tags. Assumptions that don't come off easily. Some of my best friends are sober. Some are not. The question is: *when does the labeling stop?*

We're not let off the hook for past digressions. *Ever.*

Here's my current dilemma: As a recovering addict suffering from a chronic, degenerative illness—namely Parkinson's (but imagine cancer, ALS, or anything equally merciless)—am I to be *denied* relief in the form of painkillers?

When does the patient get to say:

Enough already! Bring on the damn morphine.

As of this writing, I have Parkinson's and diabetes. It's the opposite of *Wonder Twin powers, activate.* It's hell on earth. Especially at night.

Who decides who gets pain medication and who doesn't? God? Doctors? Me?

Apparently, the answer is draconian doctors.

Since my Parkinson's diagnosis in 2022, I've pleaded and bargained.

"What if the meds are locked up and administered only by my care team?"

"Nope," says Dr. Jane Doe. "It could trigger relapse."

Depriving me, once again, of a dignified, pain-free death.

Bullcrap.

I wake up every morning in pain—if I'm fortunate enough to have slept at all. Insomnia is my nightly hell. And Dr. Jane Doe? She won't prescribe sleep meds either. Says I'm a fall risk. As if I'm not *already* falling—literally, metaphorically.

Better I be tormented by sleep deprivation than risk a spill.

Maybe I should send her a video of me pacing my house in the pre-dawn hours, startling the dog. Maybe she'd like to see me nodding off mid-conversation. Insomnia *does not* build immunity. And immunity is what I need now, more than ever.

I'm a recovering addict who *does not* want to die in pain.

Mea culpa.

More power to the people who have never taken an aspirin, who white-knuckle their way through this life.

But despite my labels—addict, alcoholic, elderly, infirm—I'm no better or worse than them.

And for today, I happen to believe that my God approves of pharmaceutical interventions.

33. ONCE AN ADDICT, ALWAYS AN ADDICT

When I think of myself as a member of the AA community, I see a good friend, someone socially aware and, in my own way, a (lowercase *p*) philanthropist. I am a worker among workers. I try to help where and how I can—bringing coloring kits to hospitals, rehabs, and detox centers to ease anxiety for people in early recovery. During the pandemic, I baked cookies for shut-ins throughout the year and for everyone I knew around the holidays. I bring candies and hearts, bunny ears and chocolate, jingle bells and cakes to meetings and friends. I drop off toys to spread a little sunshine. I want people to know they're seen and cared for.

These small gestures humble me, and they soften my heart every time. I'm proud of my standing in this community of kindred, struggling souls. But what I'm not proud of is how the medical community—at large—treats addicts.

Yes, I'm a recovering alcoholic, and I'm not afraid to say that out loud. I face life on life's terms without numbing myself with drugs or booze. My thinking is clear. I don't need a crutch to hold me up. It took almost four decades to become someone who's an upstanding member of Alcoholics Anonymous.

Yet my medical records—and my providers—remind me repeatedly that I am, in plain black print, a *substance abuser* (as in current). I haven't had an adult beverage in forty years. I am not a menace to society or to myself. But the label sticks, permanent and punishing. Here's looking at you, members of the medical profession—so quick to judge, so slow to forgive.

Over the past five years, I've been hospitalized more times than I can count. And at every single visit, without fail, someone—doctor, nurse, or employee—comments on my addiction. Not because they know me. Not because they're psychic. Because they read my chart. From that moment on, assumptions take over. I'm no longer a woman with Parkinson's, diabetes, depression, and high blood pressure. I'm a drug-seeking addict. A misfit. A liar. An unreliable narrator. A burden.

Let me say this loud and clear: my chart does not tell the whole story. It doesn't capture my recovery, my work, my heart, or my worth. I'm not just a former addict. I am a teacher, a writer, a Cal grad, a woman with master's degrees, dammit. A person who shows up for people. But too often, providers don't see beyond that single scarlet word.

Case in point: one of my doctors once referred me to a specialist. The first line in the referral? *Patient is a substance abuser.* I was immediately denied access to the new practice. When I confronted my doctor, she doubled down, claiming that addiction was my primary medical concern—above Parkinson's, above diabetes, above high blood pressure (which, for the record, was the main reason I was in her care).

I stood my ground. I told her she should feel *grateful* to serve people in recovery—people who've done the hardest work there is and come back from the brink.

I wanted to add, *Shame on you.* But she was holding my prescription, so I bit my tongue.

Once an addict, always an addict—and don't you forget it.

34. CHAR'S WALLS AT NIGHT

I'm shaking. Out of control. I can barely write. The pen refuses to do what my brain commands.

In these nocturnal panic episodes, I pivot to Lucky. He is my witness, my grounding rod. I wonder if he sees a monster in front of him. I certainly do. I am unrecognizable to myself. Hopefully, he sees some other version—the one I used to be.

I long to see her too. The girl I was. Young, wide-eyed, with the whole world stretched out in front of her. A family with means (if not emotional intelligence). A kingdom, theoretically, for the taking.

She swung for the stars—and landed flat on her ass.

In rehab.

Not once. Not twice.

Three times.

The third not being a charm, but a narrow bridge to a lesser, smaller, more contained life—free of additives and pill-fueled days.

Tonight, in this episode of *Nights with Char Char*, the nausea comes first, then the sweating, then the shaking. A trifecta of glamorous traits. I know this wave will pass—*they always do*—but when I'm in it, I feel like I'm drowning. Helpless.

I consider getting on my knees to pray, but my knees don't bend that far. If they did, I'd say:

Forgive me, God. Help me.
Help me relax.
relaX
relAX
reLAX
rELAX
RELAX.

Help me be more patient—with people, with my dog, with myself. Help me feel less trapped. Less suffocated.

I am keenly aware of Step One: I am powerless. And my life has become unmanageable.

Spinning in place, I toy with the idea of riding my stationary bike, though I know I'll turn on the TV in front of it and spiral. The world is a blazing dumpster fire and I'm already flammable. No need to add fuel.

If God were to send a coded message back, it might go like this:

Focus on the fact that your blood pressure is okay right now. You're welcome. Please give peace a chance. You're blessed. Act like it.

The attitude of gratitude has never been my natural filter. Still, I'd take the note. I'd promise to try harder. To accept the things I cannot change, yadda yadda, cue the Serenity Prayer.

By 4:12 a.m., it dawns on me: *My mental illness might defeat me.*

With that sobering thought, I want to crawl into Lucky's crate. But my walls *are* my crate. This house, this body—this life—is my container.

So why don't I feel safe inside it?

I worked so hard to make everything in this house *perfect yet commodious*. Silk curtains. Fake plants that look real. The whimsical stuffed animal here and there. Designer bags. A top-tier dog with a pedigree and a therapeutic snore.

And yet, in the end, it turned out the only imperfect thing in my carefully curated tableau, shaking, sweating, and nauseous—was me.

35. DEATH BY DONUTS

Donuts come with a price tag—and for a diabetic, the price is too high. I know this. And yet, on my way home from the hospital after a not-so-minor gallbladder removal, I found myself stage-whispering to my kind friend and driver that day, Nadine: "Pull over here. Now, please." She complied, enabling me to be non-compliant with my discharge orders.

It's not my fault that Johnny Donuts was right there, beckoning.

This wasn't my first visit to the donut rodeo that is Johnny Donuts. Not Johnny Carson. Not Johnny Cash. Johnny Donuts. I assume "Donuts" must be the owner's last name—making him Mr. Donuts. And if you haven't had Mr. Donuts' donuts, you haven't lived. On this day, it was a salted butter caramel number smothered in glaze. Four bites in under a minute. Pure bliss.

I washed it down with a sweet latte. Two no-nos. Somehow, two wrongs made it right.

Sugar is my jam. It tempts me in all forms: brownies, chocolate chip cookies, carrot cake (the best in Marin County comes from the Rustic Bakery). I haven't tried every Rustic offering, but I intend to. It's crucial for elders to have a sense of purpose.

After my first piece of Rustic carrot cake, I got inspired. I considered making my own version by peeling a carrot and slathering it with Betty Crocker icing—no skimping. But oops! I remembered: I have type 2 diabetes. Sugar, while my jam, is not my friend.

So begs the question: why do I keep self-sabotaging? What's with my urge to hasten self-destruction?

While I was falling off the wagon with my donut and latte, a server recognized me and handed me a free donut—fresh from the oven, warm and dripping with butter. It pays to be a regular. I never refuse a gift. That would be rude. I hate hurting people's feelings.

In that instant, I placed the server's feelings ahead of my own life.

I was contemplating that second donut, latte in hand, when Nadine suggested we split it—she's afraid of gaining a pound. She makes good choices. I thought this was a splendid idea. Half a donut would be only half as deadly. I'd lose only half as many minutes off my life. My blood sugar wouldn't surge above 250! All good things.

She's not a fast eater, so I went ahead and ate most of the donut. And a donut hole chaser. Who doesn't love a donut hole chaser? It would've been profligate to waste it. I washed it down with the rest of my latte. Gulp. Gulp. Gulp.

It wasn't the going down that bothered me. It was the sitting—without my gallbladder, the little engine that breaks down fats. I wondered what the surgeon did with it. They never asked if I wanted it as a keepsake.

As the donut sat swirling in latte—right where my gallbladder used to reside—I felt (and everyone heard, frankly) an explosion in my tummy. Followed by a severe reflux ache. The nausea was the worst I'd experienced in my then 78 years. It lasted all day and through the night.

My obsessive mind determined it would never go away. I was convinced I'd remain in Johnny's Donuts purgatory for the rest of my life.

Even Nadine got worried. She kept asking, "Are you okay?" I was not okay. But I tried to pretend. I was desperate to pretend.

I wanted my mother. But she was long gone.

Then I wanted God.

And in between dry heaves, I swore I heard Her whisper, "That was not a good choice, Char."

Lesson learned? For the moment.

But donuts are delicious.

And I am a flawed human being—sugar-addled and always looking for love in all the glazed places.

36. IT RUNS IN THE FAMILY

If you're born into my family—human or feline—you're likely to be chronically ill. It's the family legacy. No one gets a dramatic, tidy ending. We don't go out in a blaze of glory—we fade slowly and unglamorous. I was hoping for something terminal and quick. Instead, God and my father gave me Parkinson's.

My cat, Bruno, is similarly afflicted. He's been sick since the day he sauntered into my home looking gorgeous and doomed. His latest diagnosis? Irritable bowel syndrome. There's no cure for IBS or Parkinson's. Bruno and I are stuck, managing our unbearable, unfixable conditions like a tragic comedy duo. Why can't we both just get cancer and be done with it?

Parkinson's is treated with dopamine. But I'm not allowed to get dopamine until I wean off my antidepressant—which, they say, causes Parkinson's symptoms. I doubt that. I can't wait to start the dopamine so I can finally feel the full symptoms of dopamine. Irony is my favorite spice.

As for Bruno: his IBS is treated with steroids. Soon, my sleek, dignified feline will morph into a bloated, ravenous monster. He'll become obese (as in gluttonous) and psychotic (as in unpredictable). I wanted a pet to love—and to be lovable. Steroids don't help with that. They make animals frantic, food-driven, and slightly terrifying.

I relate. I, too, am an overeater—though without the convenient steroid excuse. My solution was Food Addicts Anonymous. It worked. I'm no longer fat. Just mentally ill. Feline variety.

There's no FAA for cats. No steroid antidote. Bruno is screwed.

Call me superficial, but I wasn't looking for a morbidly obese, mentally ill roommate.

And yet … maybe Bruno and I are soulmates. After all, in my family, misery loves company—and apparently, it runs in the bloodline.

37. HOLES, BOATS, PROMISES, ROSES

I have questions. Many questions.

For example: *When will I be comfortable in my misery? When will I fill the perma-holes in my heart and soul? Is there a prize for pain? Do I win if I'm the most miserable?*

My contemporaries and I often compare notes—and I usually win. I'd prefer a blue ribbon, which doesn't feel like an extravagant ask. And yet, the questions persist. *Do I deserve to be happy? When does my boat—named Never—come in? When will I sleep? And when, dear God, will my peers—fellow oldsters—be open and honest about this shitshow that is aging?*

I have some, but not all, of the answers.

I've learned that if you're promised a rose garden, odds are, it's not coming. You'll have to make it yourself. Life isn't something that happens to you. It's something you make.

My life has been one of privilege—I'll be the first to acknowledge that. And still, I missed the mark. The true north. It took being diagnosed with Parkinson's to let people into my life.

The Apartment Gal didn't just think small and feel small—she was also up-armored. No one really got in. I operated under the truism that to have someone is to lose someone. I don't think I'm alone in that default setting.

It's been hard-won, but I've learned to regard Parkinson's as a kind of silver lining—because it opened a world I'd always longed for: a world filled with love. Namely, the love I didn't get from my parents.

It took 78 years, countless setbacks, and an irreversible diagnosis to finally get what I wanted most from life: love and roses.

It's never too late. Life is a journey, not a destination. All the clichés are true. Run toward them.

Let your people in. Plant and embrace those seeds of beauty. And never say *Never*. Fuck that—and the boat too.

38. INQUIRING MINDS WANT TO KNOW

God, grant me the serenity to accept the things
I cannot change,
the courage to change the things I can,
and the wisdom to know the difference.
—Serenity Prayer

When you're sick—inside and out—your life is ruled by questions. I'm permanently perplexed.

Why me?

Why am I anxious, without fail, when the clock strikes six p.m.?

Why am I afraid to give myself permission to feel okay for just one minute?

When will my ruminating, future-casting, catastrophizing finally give way to gratitude, serenity, peace?

What the hell is going on with me?

My handwriting is shrinking. It's Lilliputian—perfect for wood nymphs and garden gnomes. It's also a hallmark of Parkinson's. I command my hand to write in larger letters, but it won't obey. The synapses are not synapting. (Not a word, I know—but it should be.)

More questions.

What the hell is happening to my handwriting?

What would *really* cure me is something stronger than Tylenol. But my medical brain trust, in all its collective wisdom, sticks to the placebo party line: *Take two Tylenol and call us in the morning.*

It's as if they can't hear the words behind my words.

Words like:

I want to be loved.
I want to be healthy.
I want to live.

It's been 35 years since I've been laid. They say use it or lose it. I'm afraid I've lost it.

Three and a half decades is a long time—but truthfully, I'm not altogether lonely. I have people. And for that, I'm fortunate. Romance at this age is, let's be honest, mostly overrated and anxiety-inducing for septuagenarians. Still … I know it would be fun to try.

If the opportunity arose, I'd be all in. I'd dress the part, head to toe—age-inappropriate Prada shoes, bold Johnny Was tunic—and give it a go. Before, of course, I'd have to share certain things about myself.

I'd hope the ensemble would distract him long enough to delay the inevitable inquisition:

How's your mental health? Physical health?
Any brain chemistry issues?
Mommy stuff? Daddy stuff?

There it is: one clear truth in a sea of questions.

An intimate relationship would be fun, yes—but it would also invite a whole new set of inquiries. His questions stacked on top of mine, forming a never-ending labyrinth of conversational cul-de-sacs.

Safer, for now, to stay right here. Reciting *The Serenity Prayer*. Trying to forget my family-of-origin drama and focus instead on the chosen family I've gathered—one questionably-dressed, lovingly-flawed member at a time.

39. PAIN MINUS MISSION PLUS HOPE

(A dispatch from the intersection of terrified and tired of trying.)

What really happens when you get sober?

You get *life*—whatever that entails.

In my case, that meant I got … me. In layers.

During the first decade of sobriety, I was severely depressed. Non-functional. It was suggested—by the medical cognoscenti—that I face this depression *without* drugs. So I did. For years, I sat in my LA apartment with my cats, catatonic. To their credit, they were excellent listeners. For their entertainment, I added a second act: crippling anxiety.

Staring at four walls, whispering my truth to felines, feeling safe. I stayed. For years on end.

Beneath my anxiety and depression ("A&D" in my medical chart), beneath the miasma of despair and decades of self-medicating—booze, pills, food—I was a one-woman PSA. *What Not to Do, America!* I wasn't living. I was riding out pain. It didn't suit me, but it ruled me, just like the substances that once kept it at bay.

Of all the obstacles I've faced—or created—depression is the killer. It wants you dead, or at least fantasizing about it. I still get depressed. And when it hits, it feels like a knife inside me, tearing me apart. It's not mental—it's *visceral*. It's total. And there's no such thing as "glass half empty."

There.
Is.
No.
Glass.

Enter the next gift from above: *Aging with Parkinson's*.

A familiar film reel plays in my mind. I see myself in a wheelchair. Then bedridden. Then unable to swallow or eat. The upside? In the movie, I have no memory of these losses, so I don't miss them. Until I do. Then I forget again. It's a hellish loop—grasping for memory that's already gone.

They say in AA that *God doesn't give you more than you can handle*. (A loose interpretation of 1 Corinthians 10:13, thank you, Apostle Paul.)

I'm here to say:

That guy Paul didn't have Parkinson's.

Or major depressive disorder.

Because if he had, he would've written: *God doesn't give you more than you can handle ... unless God decides you deserve a shit-ton of shit.*

Some days, I want *out*. I pray for an end. Not because I'm weak—but because I'm in pain. I don't want to die. I just want to not hurt.

The medical consensus? *What's a little pain? Better to die sober. Sobriety gets you into heaven.*

I say this to my medical team (who clearly held a meeting without me): *I'd rather take drugs and go to hell—because I'm already in hell. Is life just a test to see who can hurt the most and still survive? Please. Just give me something to kill the pain. Is that so much to ask?*

Call me a coward—I *hate* pain. I want a little mercy.

They slow-rolled me. Maybe they hoped I'd have some kind of epiphany about resilience.

Well … upon brutally honest reflection on bootstrapping:

I *may* know a way forward that doesn't require relapse.

My life in LA wasn't stellar. Sure, I was sober for 30 years. But physically and mentally, I was falling apart. My "divine life" never took shape. I pulled up stakes and moved to Northern California. *(Author reaches around and pats herself on the back.)* Best decision ever.

There, the *real* me began to emerge.

It was still a fight—every day, one day at a time. But after years of AA immersion, I got the call to serve. To help someone else.

That became my salvation.

Turns out, being of service doesn't just help *them*. It helps *me*. It gives me dopamine. It replaces all my substances—except chocolate.

That's how *The Coloring Diva* was born.

Art always helped me relax. People like me need ways to decompress. I started a program that gave people tools to color—no wrong answers, no judgment. Just pencils, paper, and peace.

It was a hit. It filled me with purpose. Until Parkinson's stepped in with its jackboot and shut it all down.

I haven't colored since my diagnosis.

But now I'm 80. Born on Valentine's Day, 2045. Time is running out.

And I plan to someday revive *The Coloring Diva.*

I don't know exactly how my final chapter will go. But I know this: The story is mine to write.

With equal parts pain, grit, humor, depression, determination—and colored pencils.

40. TO GRIEVE IS HUMAN, TO GROW IS HARDER

This missive is not meant to be a pity party. It's meant to help me process grief.

I've struggled to accept that I have Parkinson's, which is bad enough. But a friend recently stepped out of my life because of it, which is worse.

For three years, Carol was an integral part of my life: mobility trainer, garden consultant, and friend—not necessarily in that order. My therapist, a natural connector who knows everyone in our zip code, referred her to me. Still, even with the gold-plated endorsement, I was slow to warm. Unimpressed, even.

Being unimpressed may be my default defense mechanism. If I don't let people in, they can't hurt me. I see that now. After several months of circling the perimeter, I decided to give Carol a whirl.

Over time, her role blossomed, literally and figuratively—like the vines on my trellis. She helped me move and feel better. She deepened my love of gardening. Her green thumb, keen listening skills, and surprising vulnerability led to something rare: real connection.

We multitasked. Tended to my disease, my backyard, and our growing friendship—all in one go, a couple times a week. Talking about everything under the sun while nurturing roses filled me up. I felt seen. I could be myself—neuroses and all.

Then Parkinson's, that relentless thief, took another turn. Movement became painful. Sleep evaded me. Depression set in, thicker and darker. I began falling asleep mid-exercise … one, two, three, *conk.* I'd be out cold.

Naturally, our sessions became less structured and more social. I leaned on her. I depended on her.

I see now that was a mistake.

Parkinson's is a progressive disease that doesn't kill you outright. Instead, it strips your life one function at a time. Most of us die from something adjacent—like asphyxiation pneumonia. I've beaten that once. I don't know if I can beat it again. My nine lives feel nearly spent.

The point is—I didn't choose to become less mobile, or to drift off in the middle of exercises. It wasn't personal.

But eventually, in all her compassionate wisdom, Carol said she didn't want to work with me anymore.

"Since you do not seem to be up for mobility, I have no reason to continue to see you."

That was a shocker.

I had been under the illusion that we were *friends*, that our relationship was based on more than a fee-for-service exchange. I thought we had love and trust.

It felt like she bailed on me—and on the flowers—when we needed her most.

I didn't beg her to stay. I wanted her to *want* to stay. I wanted her to read my mind, then change hers.

But I was back in my shell by then. Guarded. Girded.

As my disease progresses, this will likely happen again. People will leave. I will become too much—too fragile, too exhausting, too depressing, too slow. That's the fear. That's the heartbreak.

Do I miss Carol? Of course. Do I blame her? I'm not sure.

I just know it's a terrible loss. She was an important part of my support team.

And now she is gone. Goodbye, Carol.

As I write, Lucky—the wonder dog—regards me with his unconditionally loving eyes.

Whether I'm despairing, immobile, growing or not, he has my back.

I'm grateful for that.

And for my tender roses.

41. CALLING DR. MARCUS WELBY

When my parents were elderly, their mantra was: *Find me a good doctor.*

Now that *I'm* elderly, I know exactly what they meant.

It is *not* easy finding a doctor—let alone one who is competent, compassionate, and doesn't treat you like a burden with a file number.

Someone like Marcus Welby. He made house calls, seemingly at all hours and in all weathers. His soft eyes said more than his words; his halo and humanity spoke volumes. In exchange, as patients, we regarded him as a god or at least an apostle. Granted, doctors in Dr. Welby's epoch were probably not overworked; nor did they have to contend with ruinous liability premiums or paltry insurance reimbursement rates. But still … they cared. The connection was real.

Those days are gone.

I once had a palliative doctor say, while smiling under vacant eyes, "Next time you get pneumonia, stay home."

There was also the time I called to set up a consultation with a specialist who came highly recommended by my primary care physician. After rifling off a series of short, superficial questions along the lines of *what are your concerns,* the receptionist was quick to dispatch her verdict. "I'm sorry, but you and the doctor are not a good match."

"But he hasn't even MET ME!" It's true my voice was elevated, my tone incredulous.

"Have a nice day." Click.

So much for consultations.

I know from setbacks, and this one would not deter me in my quest to find a Marin Marcus Welby. Against all odds and despite my two serious diseases with attendant complications, I finally found one. A Martha Welby if you wilI.

I liked her immediately. I was convinced she was my medical soulmate.

I was in love.

She returned calls *posthaste*. She made home visits. When I was hospitalized, she *visited me*. In person. I may not be the easiest patient (understatement), but I pay her a hefty annual fee to go above and beyond. As concierge doctors go, she's actually "affordable."

I say that because in Los Angeles, I once paid four times as much for a concierge doctor who delivered …

nothing. I was still treated like a liability. Turns out recovering addicts don't inspire a lot of empathy in the medical community—even when grossly overpaying for it.

But Dr. Martha Welby felt different. She *was* different.

Until she wasn't.

My most recent dilemma—you've heard this before but bear with me—is sleeplessness. Parkinson's and insomnia go together like peanut butter and jelly, minus the comfort or flavor. Not sleeping is *not my fault*, and neither is Parkinson's, which I won in the genetic lottery.

Naturally, I turned to my medical soulmate with a straightforward request: sleep meds. The good doctor hesitated. Understandably. Many sleep meds are potentially addictive. I understand that most doctors must be prudent when they dispense drugs to patients who *need* them versus patients who *want* them.

"I get it," I said. "But I've been clean and sober for 40 years, with one relapse seven years ago. I've got this."

She didn't look at me. She looked at her laptop before flatly refusing "I'm sorry, but no."

My once-trusted, once-dream-doctor had joined the rank and file. Punishing me for my past.

She *knows* the unrelenting sleep deprivation is destroying my life. And yet—no compassion. No creative thinking. Just "no."

She doubled down: "So what? You don't sleep for a couple of days. Eventually, you'll fall asleep."

"Not true," I countered. "And what about my depression? I'm at my wit's end."

That's when she offered her final prescription: Kindly, calmly, and in so many words, she suggested I go home and stop eating, offering me a slow, painful way out of life.

"Maybe then, you will sleep."

I may have misheard her. Or maybe I didn't. Either way, message received.

Thus, I'm prioritizing a new search. A good doctor. Just like my parents once did.

Full circle.

42. MY LITTLE VOICE

I'm going to share this, and I know it's heresy. Don't tell anyone.

I don't believe in God.

Well—that's not entirely true.

I'd define myself more as a *tangible agnostic*. If I can't see God sitting across the breakfast table, He doesn't exist.

Pass the butter buster—or better yet, levitate it to me.

At best, I'm conflicted about belief in a higher power.

Descartes said, "I think, therefore I am."

I say, "I think, therefore I am … confused."

My higher power doesn't carry a staff or resemble Santa Claus. He's centered inside me, near my heart. During crucial moments, he tells me what to do—not with a shout, but a whisper. *Sotto voce*. He is my protector.

Or maybe *she* is. Doesn't matter. This quiet, unwavering voice always shows up when I'm at a crossroads. It never steers me wrong.

Doubt me? I have proof.

When I was born, I cried at the sight of my mother—perfect makeup, polished nails, coiffed hair. My little voice said: *This is who I'm sending you to … good luck.*

I had my own bedroom next to my only sibling—a brother. My inner voice whispered: *Stay away. He wants nothing to do with you.*

Eighty years later, the voice is still right about him. I invited him to my 80th birthday. He declined. Like my parents, he's an emotional well run dry. My work now is to stop taking it personally after a lifetime of taking it personally.

I would've gotten more love squeezing a turnip than I ever got from my family of origin. A turnip doesn't reject you. My family did. They transformed an adorable, loving little girl into a depressed child-turned-adolescent-turned-addict.

For years, I lost my little voice. Should I go right? Left? Stay in Berkeley? Transfer to UCLA? Rush a sorority? Live with my parents—who turned my childhood bedroom into a den within weeks of my leaving for college?

I had no idea. I made bad choices. I stayed at UCLA—a lonely fish in a deep pool of beautiful peers who looked past me. I had no real friends. Just a therapist I paid to listen to my sanitized bullshit.

My abusive boyfriend certainly didn't qualify. He once insisted I walk ten feet behind him. It was a painful, lonely time, and I coped the only way I knew how: with drugs. I submerged myself in Valium and opiates for over 20 years, silencing my voice until it died completely. No rudder. No direction. Just pills.

I did everything wrong.

I stayed in L.A. too long, until I nearly died. Not an exaggeration.

At 35, as foreshadowed, I drove my car into *two* parked cars in a blackout. I was ungovernable. I went to the hospital and treated myself—with more drugs.

Three very long years later, I heard my little voice again. It said: *You've had enough. This is your rock bottom.*

I listened, with gratitude, and marched my ass to an AA meeting, where I felt at home. I fit in. I exhaled. Inhaled. Connected. This was my place, and these were my people. They'd been there and back and some of them, let's be real, made me seem like a goody two shoes.

When I left, a woman followed me out.

"Are you an alcoholic?"

"No, but I'm addicted to Valium. Does that count?"

"It does," she said. "And so do you."

Kind eyes. Open heart. She handed me a slip of paper from her purse. "Call me."

I did. The next day. I half-expected a bill. But she didn't charge me. She helped me—for free.

This was new. A first.

Through her, I learned I couldn't go it alone. I tried to get into a residential treatment program. No luck.

You know the old saying: when the going gets tough, the tough call their mother.

After years of distance, I called mine. I told her I wanted to get sober and needed money for rehab. I knew she didn't know what "rehab" meant.

"I'll call your father," she said, flatly.

She called back moments later: "Your father said yes."

That night, I was admitted to the St. Jude's Chemical Dependency Ward. I took my little yellow buddies—Valium—from my pocket and flushed them down the toilet.

Never again, I vowed.

The doctors didn't think I'd stay sober. "Too far gone," the case notes said.

But my little voice knew better.

And so did I—for the next thirty years. Until I relapsed on opiates and headed back to rehab.

Where was my little voice then?

At long last, in 2017, just when I was nearing the end of my rope—driving the hills of San Rafael—it returned. Crystal-clear: *You really want to live here.* And I did. A whisper in my soul that turned everything around.

Call it divine intervention.

43. MENDING AND TENDING TO ME

Relocating to NorCal healed me on many levels.

The years in my new environs have been the best years of my life. I got sober. I lost 40 pounds. As mentioned, I created *The Coloring Diva*—a project that offered free coloring kits to people dealing with anxiety and depression. A small thing, maybe, but a proven form of art therapy. A soothing, healthy addiction. A tool in the angsty artist's toolbox.

I distributed kits across the county, through my AA network and various nonprofits. It felt good to give. It felt good to make a difference.

Then Parkinson's came along and stomped on my *Coloring Diva* initiative. Just flattened it.

Today, my focus is on keeping the inexorable symptoms at bay. And so, for the first time in my life, I'm giving myself a pass. Permission to pause. To tend to me.

I have faith that my little voice will guide me again—when the time is right, and all the way to my final chapter.

Disease or no disease, these *are*—and will continue to be—the best years of my life. I try to remember that with every turn, every setback, every obstacle.

After all, a brand-new year always promises new beginnings—for everyone, even little old me.

44. MY SCARS WERE ON THE INSIDE

January 20, 2025

I always wanted to be a baby boomer.

I missed it by about a year.

My whole life is a series of misses. But to be a boomer? That might've solved everything. Boomers, as AI will cheerfully inform you, are known for their strong work ethic, optimism, focus on personal achievement, and engagement in social movements.

Instead, I was born into a silenced cohort of one.

For a long time, I thought my name was *Shut up.*

When I asked my father a question, his answer was always the same: "Shut up."

It was *shut up this* and *shut up that*, all day, every day.

A typical Saturday morning:

Me (age 7): “Daddy, can we go to the park?”

Him (not glancing up from his newspaper): “Shut up.”

Me at a fundraiser or backyard BBQ: “Daddy, can I have ice cream?”

Him (half-turning, mid-chat with someone important): “Shut up and go find your brother.”

I was an interruption. An inconvenience.

If I popped up into his line of vision, it was: “Oh, it’s *you* again. What do you want?”

“Nothing,” I’d mumble, eyes down, swallowing my words, my wants, my dreams.

And I stayed that way. Silent Char.

Only our dog Freckles, a Springer spaniel with bloodshot eyes, listened. Those eyes said everything: *I love you no matter what, Silent Char.*

When Freckles wasn’t out impregnating every unspayed dog in the neighborhood, he was nestled next to me on the cold kitchen linoleum. I'd wrap my arms around his belly and breathe with him, both of us rising and falling. He had conquered the world—or at least the block. I had stayed stuck.

Fear and anxiety pinned me in place.

But here's the irony: when my friends were sprouting pimples by the dozen, my skin was flawless. Not a blemish. No acne.

My scars were on the inside.

In all the years my father was alive, he never once called me, sent a card, or gave me a gift.

His one day off, Sunday, followed the same rigid schedule:

— Wake up early
— Water the garden
— Sweep the sidewalk
— Spray down the patio furniture
— Make lunch
— Wash his dishes
— Lock himself in his study until dinner

At dinner, he emerged, ate silently, then vanished again behind that door. He didn't need a *Do Not Disturb* sign—his energy said it all:

Do not disturb me.
You are a hindrance.
I do not want you.
You are a mistake.
Try not to be seen. And never be heard.

I took that ball and ran with it—straight into isolation, addiction, and more silence.

A generation of one.

But hopefully not done.

45. ON THE TOPIC OF SELF-HARM

Sept. 30, 2017

The writer's job, says Jonathan Franzen, is to "say the unsayable."

I aspire to do just that.

After pain plagued me for countless years, I began to like making myself hurt even more. I must I hate myself for continuing to do this. For digging my nails into my skin, over and over. And yet, I persist.

For me—and for 5% of adults, 17% of adolescents, and up to 35% of college students in America—this sickness is soothed by pain. No science can fully explain it. It's not logical. It's emotional.

And now, at least, it's honest.

No one talks about it. It's taboo. So let me go there.

I pick my skin. Until it bleeds. I dig my index nail into my outer thigh, over and over, forming a callus. Then I dig deeper into the callused skin. That callused thigh of mine? It's my comfort object. Not a pink baby blanket. Not my mother's handkerchief, scented with Chanel No. 5.

This is *my* kind of comfort. Self-destructive soothing, born of self-hatred.

And still. I. Can't. Stop.

I once walked the Los Angeles Marathon in 8.5 hours, as if time itself were chasing me and my battered thighs. I am proud of that long, brisk walk. It hurt, but it also healed something.

The clock ticks. The sand runs through the hourglass. This is *no* time for secrets.

I want anyone who self-harms to know this:

You are not alone.
Life hurts. We do our best—
even if our best is yet to come.

46. A PLACE FOR PAIN

A Place for Mom—you've seen the ads, right? They offer in-home care services for your beloved, if not doddering and diminishing, mother—whom you would prefer to outsource, thank you very much, because you're busy living your best life (no thanks to said mother).

I never had to make that difficult decision. My dearest mommy—a Jewish woman with the sensitivity of a Nazi Schutzstaffel guard—went out on her own terms. No nursing homes. No casseroles. No long goodbyes.

But recently it occurred to me: while I never needed *A Place for Mom*, I've spent my life cultivating *A Place for Pain*. I've built it, swept its floor, fluffed its pillows. I've even decorated.

Here's what I wrote in my journal, September 2017:

The issue today is abandonment. No, that's not right—the issue is anger. The day has turned into night, and time is running out, and my anger is stuck in my leg, masquerading as pain. Rather than let it rip, I turn my anger inward, cradling it—a commodity I can't sell, but I can transmute it (like Christ!) into pain. Having not been allowed to express anger in my family-of-origin home—a home that was mostly silent, lined with eggshells and hollow hearts—that emotion remains baked in the cake. It must live somewhere, so why not my leg?

That's where I housed it. Not in conversation, not in a therapist's office, not even in a scream. I housed it in my flesh.

I fed it with silence.

I made room for it.

Sometimes, healing means evicting what you've grown used to living with—for good.

47. HELP FROM ABOVE, WITHOUT AND WITHIN AND REALITY STILL WINS

Dispatch from 2023

I have the Third Step Prayer on repeat in my mind, the gist of which is to get out of one's own way and start doing my Higher Power's good work on this earth, in this life. It's my anchor. And yet ... I self-sabotage. Why can't I just relax? I know enough to know that acceptance is the solution to all my problems.

Take this, for example: If I could simply accept that I'm old and need caregivers—most of whom are kind, except when they're not—maybe I'd have more peace. I won't name names. Okay, I will: it was Jaime (not his real name; he knows who he is). He betrayed me, yes—but he betrayed himself first.

Chad, my weekly massage therapist (bless him for making house calls), recently declared that the fascia in my feet and calves is tight. This tracks, given that my feet are often numb. Numbness, it turns out, doesn't always require drugs. In old age, the body takes over.

Maybe it's my body's way of saying, *I need space. I'm maxed out.* I've got my superhero dog and Wendall, my right-hand man. I love them both. But it's enough.

I'm proud of the fact that while I walk like an oldster, I don't (yet) need a cane. I despise canes. Too on-the-nose. A literal crutch. As in: *I can't make it through this life—from room to room or place to place—without leaning my heavy heart on something.* No, thank you.

I will concede that my memory is fading (Charlene who?) which is partly why I'm trying to get it all down—on the page, in print. A life, memorialized.

The indignities of aging are legion. The gift that keeps on giving. Have I mentioned that my neck is stiff? What does that mean? What does it represent? It hurts when I bend to write. I'm at odds with myself most of the time—especially when I'm trying to be productive. What would Freud say about that?

He'd have a field day with my anxiety. I know when my blood pressure spikes—my neck locks up. I become a corpse with a beating heart. Motionless. Depressed. Shot through with pain.

From age 50 to 65, I dodged these aches and pains with antipsychotic meds I took every morning. I genuflected at the altar of Big Pharma. It was a time-limited relationship, one that would eventually succumb to reality.

For my remaining years, I'll remember this: We are all perfectly imperfect—and worth it.

And I'll keep asking myself: Why not get out of our own way, sideline the ghosts of the past, and embrace the day?

48. MY MOTHER'S LIFE IN OUNCES

Everything in my mother Dorothy's life was measured: emotions, status, her food, the dog's food, my food, her pills.

Breakfast was Melba toast, black coffee, and a cholesterol pill. The pill was blue, which probably soothed her, as it matched the blue velvet furniture in her perfectly curated, blue-themed condo.

She ate ten carrots for lunch. Never nine. Never eleven.

The dinner hour commenced with a martini—her way of calming down after a full day of salon appointments (nails don't maintain themselves, people), cutting camellias, and counting out the kibble for her compliant poodle.

Everyone in Dorothy's life, come to think of it, was compliant. They had to be. She wouldn't tolerate emotional—or any other kind of—disarray. Millie the maid, Andy the poodle, and Jacob the son all understood the rules.

If you weren't compliant, you were held at arm's length. And then, eventually, expelled.

And honestly?

They were the lucky ones.

49. AND YET I STILL WANT TO BE FAMOUS

My mother gifted me, genetically, with a sense of style and ... actually, that's about it.

Oh wait—she also gave me the fear gene. She was governed by it. A full-time slave to fear. That's something we shared. From the moment I shot out of her chute (yes, that's what she called it—like a ride at Six Flags Magic Mountain), fear became both my lodestar and the albatross around my neck.

From my father, Paul, I inherited thin hair, blue eyes, and a love of potato chips—something that helped usher in my diabetes. He had it, I have it. We shared that inheritance too.

He also ran the full-on family show. Director, writer, star. He was some strain of tyrant—the kind who kicks a child in the ribs for not doing the dishes. (I will never forget that day.)

If this were a screenplay, my father—aka *The Controller*—would've done the casting.

My feeding-tube-thin mother would be the protagonist, stifled by her burdensome children. A golden boy (perfect) and a problem girl (imperfect). The boy would go on to crush college. The girl would go on to crush benzos. The boy's crowning achievement? A PhD. The girl's? Beating David Feldstein in the sixth-grade spelling bee.

The girl would show up late to the set, likely high on doctor-approved opioids, wearing a Neiman Marcus cashmere sweater and a dazed expression. She would have recently devoured a bag of Famous Amos cookies, leaving her with high-octane gas, heartburn, and acid reflux—which she'd battle with Gas-X, Nexium, and Tums.

And that's when the show would end. Before it ever began.

Despite this family drama debacle and my fear-based wiring, *a la* generational trauma, I've always loved a stage. Which is why, once upon a delusional time, I took an improv class.

I had aspirations.

To be famous.

Still do.

50. TO BE FAMOUS WHILE ORDINARY: A QUESTION AND A FANTASY

We're born alone, we live alone, we die alone. Only through our love and friendship can we create the illusion for the moment that we're not alone.
—Orson Welles

When I was a young lass, all I wanted was to be famous.

Not a mother. Not a wife. Just *famous*.

I didn't crave children or a picket fence—I wanted *fame* after my name. To be seen.

Noticed. Recognized. I was none of those things in my family of origin, so it's not surprising that I yearned for attention despite being erased.

As life unfolded (or unraveled), I never married. Never had kids. Never became famous. Unless you count that one improv class I sleepwalked through in my twenties.

Now, as a newly minted octogenarian—with no husband to grow old with and no grandchildren to adore—I finally realize *I matter.* My point of view matters.

That's always been true, of course. I just didn't know it.

I wanted to be a famous journalist.

Didn't happen.

Tried writing sitcoms.

No dice.

Dreamed of becoming a world-renowned therapist like Dr. Phil.

Didn't even get the mustache.

What I *didn't* want to be known for:

- Hitting two parked cars while in a blackout.
- Being wheeled into the ER after overdosing.
- Needing not one, not two, but *three* rehabs to finally get sober.
- Being *that woman* at AA who, against all odds, never got a DUI. (Applause, please?)

Yet here I am. Somehow, still standing. Still sober. Still dreaming.

And yes—I know my chance of becoming famous is right up there with winning the lottery.

But I emailed Oprah anyway. YOLO, right?

I'm ordinary.

Can an ordinary person still claim a little fame?

Maybe not. But I swapped out my birth family for a chosen one in the hopes of being seen, and sometimes, that's enough.

If nothing else, I'd like my tombstone to read:

Charlene Kodimer lies here.
An ordinary woman whose claim to fame was that she was never seen—until she was.

But honestly? I'm not going down without a little razzle-dazzle.

Provided I've got a few bucks left when I go, I plan to hire 1,000 extras to attend my funeral. They'll line up to say glowing things about me. Sure, they'll be paid. Sure, I'll be dead.

But I will not go quietly or without a celebrity-caliber party.

#notdeadyet #nonamefame

51. PRAY. ACT. REPEAT

It took me a while to figure it out, but I learned that the best way to take my pain away was to take *action*.

Here's my three-step recipe for recovery—short, imperfect, and lifesaving:

Step 1: Pray.
Whatever "prayer" looks like to you—ask for help.
Surrender. Whisper into the void. Just begin.

Step 2: Act.
This is the essential step. Without action, nothing changes.
You don't grow. You don't give. And it turns out—it *feels good* to grow and contribute. Who knew? I didn't.

Step 3: Repeat.
As often as needed. Start again. Then start again.

When *enough* was finally enough—and we each know in our heart when that moment comes.

When I was exhausted, out of excuses, and had one foot in the grave … I stepped back from the cliff.

I didn't do it alone. It took an AA village.

And I thank God every day for that village.

My hope for you is this: that you don't have to get to that point. But if you do, there's still a way back.

Pray. Act. Repeat.

52. HOW CHARLENE ESCAPED HER WALLS

2025

I'm not a risk-taker. I never have been. Walking around the block in Marina del Rey felt dangerous. Returning to my apartment wasn't much better—just a different kind of danger: the kind called loneliness.

And yet—somehow, late in life—I packed up and left Los Angeles.

I drove north, alone, over the Golden Gate Bridge, headed toward the mysterious hinterlands of Marin County. I was a septuagenarian with a suitcase and a sliver of hope. Where I found the courage to do this, I'll never know. But I did it. And I never looked back.

As fate would have it, I remained lonely for a while—but at least I wasn't alone in *that*. A 2024 poll by the American Psychiatric Association found that 30% of American adults experience loneliness at least once a week. In my case, it was more like once a minute. It sucked the life force right out of me.

All I ever wanted was to be seen, hugged, loved. But I had built a fortress around myself—one no one could scale.

Until something shifted. Marin cracked me open. And into that tiny crack stepped Lexie. I paid her to be my sleep buddy (insomnia is a cruel mistress), but over time, we became friends. Real friends.

Letting her in was a calculated risk. But when you've got nothing left to lose, even calculated risks can feel like leaps of faith.

Lexie led to more introductions. More connections. And eventually—to my great surprise—a real, meaningful life. A life with fun, kind, compassionate people who see me.

And those walls?

I left them in L.A.

53. MOVE OVER ENEMY # 1

July 2025

Today, I'm very likely somatizing (Greek word) pain in my back, neck, and head. This is a pattern. Whenever I get close to making a big change—like finishing my book—my body revolts. The pain becomes so intense, I incapacitate myself. It's my superpower, apparently.

Case in point: that fateful night before my big, post-grad school job interview when I downed copious amounts of Valium. I feel like doing that again. Instead, I'm writing.

I'm full of fear—as evidenced by my high blood pressure and recent affair with the fridge. I am my own worst enemy. Enemy #1: Charlene Kodimer. When I was in my 30s and started writing TV scripts, I submitted them to producers. My back promptly gave out. So I concluded—courtesy of me—that my writing career was over. I quit before I even got started.

I'm scared again. But now I'm sober, and I have a program. I need to work the steps, face the fear of getting what I want: to be a successful writer with a twist of humor. The opposite of fear is faith, and that's what I need now. Tons of it.

I'd do well to remember: God doesn't make junk. He made me. And I'm certainly not junk.

This I know to be true: When I stopped blaming my family of origin for everything—including my own decisions—I made space for a new family, one step at a time. Risk-taking wasn't in my blood, but I did it anyway. That was progress. It saved my life.

But not at first. When I was in the SoCal soup, I didn't know how deep I was because I was too busy pretending I was fine. It's no surprise that my first run at sobriety didn't last—soul-crushing loneliness is hard to beat. I had to get out to look back and finally move forward. The second time I got sober—in my new, adopted NorCal—it stuck.

The path wasn't linear. I bounced from one rehab to another, one SLE to another, one rental to another. But shazam—four years into Marin living, I found my dream house. True to form, I nearly pulled out of escrow. But I took the leap. After much planning and effort, it has become an expression of the new me: small, elegant, stylish, and mostly welcoming. Orchids. Figurines. And, of course, the beloved dog, Lucky, who is more than welcome on all the furniture (because, thank God, I am *not* my mother).

Thanks to my chosen family and this community, I feel loved. Blessed. Not lonely—for the first time in my life. What L.A. always lacked, NorCal has in spades.

Yes, I have Parkinson's. And yes, it's hard. Some days all I can do is lie on the couch in pain. Other days, I go to meetings, meet friends for lunch, even exercise. The worst days are a wash. I miss out on the very things that bring me joy. But I'm blessed—I have 24/7 caregivers who are more like family. They attend to my needs and support my hopes and dreams however they can.

Living with a chronic illness would be unbearable alone. But I’m not alone. I belong to several 12-Step groups that help me grow—and push me out of my comfort zones—even when I occasionally fall asleep mid-share (sometimes upright)! The point is, I show up. Again and again. And that consistency is part of what keeps Enemy #1 at bay.

In Marin, I’ve discovered the real me. I can be funny, generous, and someone who helps others through their pain. Do I still occasionally crave massive amounts of drugs and doughnuts? Absolutely. But those thoughts have become fewer and farther between. I can always find gratitude here—in this gorgeous little pocket of the world. I even hug the cashiers at my favorite Mediterranean restaurant. They hug me back. Sometimes they comp my meal.

I've swapped booze—and a thousand other crutches Enemy #1 relied on—for Fattoush salads and familiar smiles. I'm no longer The Apartment Gal, lost, alone, and desperate. I’m becoming a *Large Yam*—an independent woman with an unapologetically large life.

I have changed. For good. And I am eternally grateful.

54. 80TH BIRTHDAY GIFT FROM MY BROTHER

I always wanted an older brother but never had one—until now.

It took 80 years, but he was worth the wait.

Let me explain.

My earliest recollection of my brother is one of yearning. I longed for a sibling who would love me, play with me, take me under his wing. But by age three, I knew I'd get none of that. He kept me at arm's length—even as a toddler. He was modeling our parents. He wanted nothing to do with me. There was no safe harbor, no tenderness, no attention.

So, I did what any child without power might do: I broke all his toys. Sweet revenge. One day, I snuck into his room and snapped all his precious crayons in half. No more coloring for him. Of course, I was punished. I didn't care. Totally worth it.

Still, shortly after that transgression, he invited me to play gas station. I should have known. He flipped his bicycle upside down, and I stuck my finger into the spinning chain. He turned the wheel. Voilà—no finger. My brother insists he was more distraught than I was. Maybe. But I was the one bleeding.

To her credit, my mother rushed me to the doctor and made sure I kept all my digits. No child of hers could be less than perfect—she'd see to that.

Years later, having *somewhat* repaired our dynamic, my brother and I ran away from home. Our destination: Aunt Renée's house in glamorous Beverly Hills—a definite upgrade from our modest suburb. She had a pool.

My brother led the charge on his Schwinn. I followed on my red, sparkly tricycle with steely (read: temporary) determination. We made it as far as the railroad tracks before I burst into tears. I missed my mommy. I wanted to go home. My brother, resolute, wanted to press on. My tears won.

We returned home to Mother's famously closed-off, non-embrace. Her arms remained pinned to her sides. She offered no comfort. My brother was pissed. Another betrayal. No swimming that day. I'd let him down—again.

Still, I clung to the hope that he might one day love and protect me. That hope faded. I redirected my affection to dogs. They didn't push me away. They didn't shame me. They just loved me.

By age twelve, I was depressed, withdrawn, retreating from a world that didn't want me. That default to isolation lasted decades. When that didn't work, I turned to addiction. A good girl gone numb. Drugs, sugar, silence.

Where was my brother in all this? AWOL. He had his own axe to grind. When he married an Asian woman, our parents disowned him. He didn't blink. He got a PhD and became a neuropsychologist. If breaking things was my rebellion, becoming a man was his.

Family lore: he built, I destroyed.

He got a happy ending: wife, child, career.

I got mine (much) later: pet, garden, healing.

Over the years, he stuck to his life of schedules, golf and hard lines. He had little room for his messy sister with too many needs, too many crocodile tears, too much everything. Every time I reached out for help, he wasn't there. A brother in name only. I resented him—but mostly I hurt. And I was out of toys to break.

When I most recently got sober, having moved to Marin and founding *The Coloring Diva*, I began to shine. For the first time, I felt whole. No Prada shoes or Gucci purse necessary—just roses, real friends, healthy (if boring) food, art, words, and Lucky, my ever-loving dog. That's the life I'd always longed for.

Note: nowhere in that list is my brother.

I'd long painted him as the antagonist of my childhood and an absentee adult. We now live miles apart—my NorCal to his SoCal. But something has shifted. We talk on the phone, semi-regularly. I asked him to come to my 80th birthday. He declined—no surprise, no disappointment.

But then he said something that knocked my socks off: "We have a great and meaningful relationship, even if it's only over the phone."

With those words I realized: he's been there. Just not in the way I needed him to be. He has limits. I'm a hugger, a feeler, a show-up-at-your-door kind of sibling. He's not. His love is relayed in phone calls. I've come to respect that.

So here I am—in the *phone zone*. Compare: friend zone, sister zone, love-you-from-afar zone. And that must be good enough.

As our call was ending, I went for it.

"I love you," I said.

"I love you too," he said back.

A first.

And the best birthday gift I've ever received.

Even if it did take 80 years.

Thank you, bro. 

55. WORDS TO THE WISE

On the verge of my Valentine's Day 80th birthday, here's what I know:

- The grass is not always greener—especially on the hard days. But remember, there are *many* shades of green. Embrace your colors, your moss, kelly, opal, emerald, mint, hunter, chartreuse. All shades of you.

- Money won't make you happy—but it *can* be used to wipe away tears.

- Addiction, in any form, ruins your life.

- Whomever said friends weren't important didn't have any.

- It's not easy to let go of the past—but it's harder to keep dragging it behind you.

- Always play hard to get. It's more attractive. And more fun.

- If someone hurts your feelings, don't take it personally. It's about *them.*

- Sharing is caring—unless it's a bribe.

- You don't choose your family. After that, it's up to you.

- When you're depressed, take a pill.
When you're not depressed... take a pill?
(Oops—forgot I'm in AA.)

- Separation anxiety is real. Cutting the apron strings is a bitch.

- Ken and Barbie are not real. Neither is Instagram.

- The opposite of *FEAR* is *FAITH*—unless you're a coward. Then have a Twinkie.

- Always follow your dreams. Even if you trip over them now and then.

- It's never too late. Don't quit before the miracle.

- Your parents are never as bad as you think—
unless they are.

- Blondes have more fun. Redheads, however, have *the most* fun.

- I tried it (whatever *it* was). It didn't help.

- Plastic surgery *can* improve your self-esteem—but it depends on the surgeon.

- Straight A's don't count in hospice.

- It's better to have loved and lost than never to have loved at all.
(But have you *seen* the divorce rate?)

- I should've married my seventh-grade boyfriend, Adam Goldberg. At twelve, he was kind, attentive, and funny. He became a doctor. Even my parents would've approved.
Hold on to the keepers.

- Loneliness kills.

- Honesty is the best policy. Unless you're in government.

- Don't cry over spilled milk—unless it's chocolate.

56. I'M 80!

I threw myself a spectacular party when I turned 80—even hired a fabulous local band. Here's what I told my guests that night:

Below is my toast on that occasion.

Ross, California saved my life. Thank God for Ross.

When I landed here, I had just relapsed after 30 years of sobriety. I was wasting away—slowly dying, really—in Marina del Rey. I had spent a lifetime there, disconnected and depleted.

Just as I was born into the wrong family, I was living in the wrong city. Los Angeles fit my parents to a tee—all their perfect, polished square pegs clicked into perfect, polished square holes. But me? I didn't fit. No matter how hard I tried, I didn't belong.

I was a misfit. I tried on every size, every role—grad student, journalist, sitcom writer. None of it fit. The schools weren't right, the jobs weren't right, and (here's looking at you Gary, Jeff, Alan, Michael, Ken) the men weren't right. Still, I stayed. I was stuck in a lonely, addicted life until I was 70 years old—and I never even thought to leave.

And I'm not even to the bad part yet.

Sometimes it takes a split-second decision to bring us into the light. My late-in-life relapse was yet another rock bottom. But a psychiatrist I barely knew said, "Go to Harbor Hill." I had no other options, which turned out to be a blessing. A *God shot.*

Remember—I didn't belong. But the moment I drove over the Golden Gate Bridge, something shifted. For the first time in 70 years, I belonged. I not only fit, I felt *home.*

I knew, deep in my bones, that I wanted to live here. I never looked back. I never returned to Los Angeles—except to sell my house and haul my designer shoes and purses up to Marin. A girl must keep her priorities straight.

Transplanting myself here led me to a community of loving souls—namely, *you.* All of you in this room. This place, and these friends, helped me start becoming the woman I was meant to be.

Since arriving in Marin, I've worn many hats: The Coloring Diva. The Doughnut Queen. The Snack Lady. What can I say—I express myself through food and felt tips.

It's still a journey. But I believe the best is yet to come.

I'm not happy all the time— *lol!* —but now I have a glass that's half full. Well ... maybe not every day, but at least I *have* a glass. In L.A., I had no glass. Just a whole lot of heavy, dated baggage.

Most importantly: I am no longer lonely. You, my chosen family, have filled my heart.

You've transformed me. You've made me whole.

I thank you for walking this road with me—and for being my friends.

Who knew that driving myself to rehab over the Golden Gate Bridge would eventually lead me here?

To my 80th birthday.
To all of *you.*
To this band!
Tonight, my glass overflows with love.
And I thank you.
Let's dance!

57. STEP ONE TO BECOMING A YAM: ASK "WHAT CAN I DO FOR YOU?"

Some people—me included—just need a lift.

When pills, puppies, and Waterford crystal stopped elevating my soul, I tried something new: giving.

I started small. I made it my mission to put a smile on the face of everyone I encountered. Not easy. Some people are determined to stay sour and dour. (I should know—I was one of them.)

But I persisted. Then I took it a step further.

I began putting the needs of others ahead of my own—not in a martyr-y way, but with intention. That shift changed everything. It wasn't just a strategy to escape my own gloom; it turned out to be the key to real connection. To something that felt like meaning.

It was liberating. My proverbial cup, once cracked and dry, began to fill.

People replaced things.

Emotions replaced repression.

Generosity of spirit supplanted grasping for petty wants and "needs."

You first replaced *me first*.

To this day, I try to lead with that lens. I start each day asking:

What can I do for someone else?

When I do, I'm well on my way to becoming a YAM. A human one, not the tuber.

58. DEAR OPRAH: LET'S BE FRIENDS!

Everyone knows Oprah. Like Cher, Prince, and Cleopatra, she just has the one name: Oprah.

I have two. Charlene and Kodimer. Yep—two. How much more famous can you get?

But Charlene Kodimer? I've never even heard of me.

I was tangential at birth. My mother was too busy preparing for her hospital exit. Her needs eclipsed those of her newborn daughter.

Foreshadowing. She always took precedence.

Fast forward 80 years later: still two names, still not famous. The future is not what you'd call promising—unless you consider a colonoscopy a red-carpet event.

Still, I haven't given up.

Short of legally deleting my last name (and confusing the DMV, my pharmacist, and most of my AA group), I've decided to reach out to Oprah. Why not?

We all know Gayle—note the missing last name—is Oprah's best friend. But maybe Oprah's lonely. Maybe she wants *another* friend. (How gracious of me, I know.)

I could use a friend too. Why not Oprah? As I always say: start at the top.

Here's how my breezy letter will go:

Hi Oprah,

I'm reaching out to offer you something rare: the friendship of a slightly worn, occasionally wise, still-kinda-sparkly octogenarian.

If it gets lonely up there in the stratosphere, I'm here. I think we'd have a great time swapping stories—especially about people who live in L.A. (I know you have thoughts.)

If you're too busy to answer—or already drowning in besties—or if Gayle might get friendvy (friend envy)—I'll understand.

With love and weird optimism,

Your new bestie,

Charlene

P.S. If you've read this, O, I've officially dropped the last name. Just one name now. Maybe you can aim for just one letter? We can process over coffee.

59. LUCKY

Like all good humans, I've had many pets. My track record, however, is mixed. I probably inherited this trait from my mother, whose dogs never fared well under her cold, watchful eye and stone-hearted supervision.

Blinky was my first. His head bobbed, his tail wagged, he barked and walked a few feet before tipping over. No matter. I dragged him down sidewalks by his leash like a proud seven-year-old. He didn't mind being pulled on his side for blocks at a time. Loyal, if a little lifeless. The dealbreaker? His batteries died every couple of weeks. Defective. Disappointing. I grieved for a day, then demanded a *real* dog.

My mother said no. *She'd* be the only one in the family with a dog. Ever.

As fate dictates, the minute I moved into a pet-friendly two-bedroom apartment, I got my own damn dog and gave Daisy her own room. I was already crushing it as a first-time dog mama.

Was I capable of taking care of myself, let alone an animal? No. But I didn't know that yet. Neither did Daisy.

I did all the performative good-dog-owner things. I even laid down pee pads in her room. She peed in every *other* room instead. Day and night.

For solace and support, I turned to my best friends: benzos. Dr. Kaplan, my easily manipulated prescriber, made sure I had a steady stream. I own my choices—but I still wonder if he knew *exactly* what he was doing.

As the drugs dulled and failed, I sought distraction. A new backdrop. I applied to grad school in journalism at USC. Miracles happen. Active addiction didn't stop me from doing well in classes—I got Bs, all while looking cute in shirtdresses, sans bra. 'Twas the time. (For those keeping score: that's a B in academics, and an A in sartorial sexy—which is an A in my book.)

I floated. I avoided. I coped. Meanwhile, Daisy floundered. I didn't walk her. I felt guilty. I took more pills.

When graduation neared and the pressure to find a job mounted, I leaned into the life skills I'd refined over time. Just kidding. I took more pills.

Remember: I was the girl who wasn't even allowed in the kitchen to make a peanut butter and jelly sandwich. When it came time to fly out for a Very Important On-Camera Journalism Job Interview (read: Life or Death), I missed the flight. Too many pills the night before.

A perfect self-sabotage dismount, brought to you by Dr. Kaplan and me. Joint effort.

Goodbye, Barbara Walters. Hello, Amy Winehouse.

My promising career in journalism evaporated that day. I chose the path of least persistence. My parents looked away, content to keep sending money if I didn't disrupt their carefully curated lives with my inconvenient drama.

I stayed in that apartment for years, curtains drawn, lights off, dog untrained. My primary exercise: lifting pills to my mouth. I watched daytime TV. Daisy, years later, went blind, stumbled off a sidewalk, and died ten feet from me. It wasn't my fault—but I thought it was. I sobbed as I scooped her up. This was L.A., so no one broke stride, much less offered to help.

I stayed Amy Winehouse for years. I wasn't dead, but I wanted to be—though not until I hit my ideal weight of 120 pounds. I've always been practical.

Flash forward. Many years. Many attempts at pets—Cookie, Mollie, Bruno. Each of them: perfectly imperfect. As my 80th birthday approached, I wanted one last try. No batteries. No puppy problems. Just a soulful companion.

Sober now, and finally embracing my inner perfectionist, I perused *400* doggie magazines. When I saw *the one*, his eyes locked with mine, right off the page. "Howie" was calling to me. *Bow wow. Ruff, ruff. Take me home.*

I contacted the owner immediately.

He was adamant: *Howie isn't right for you.*

I rebelled.

"I'm never wrong about anything—especially animals. I want Howie!" Was my voice elevated? Slightly panicked? Absolutely.

He acquiesced—but not how I expected.

"I have a better match for you. I'm certain. Flawless specimen. A Cavalier King Charles Spaniel."

"I doubt it."

"Trust me," he said, smugly.

Then he texted a photo.

As a good Jew, I never surrender. But I surrendered. I melted. I named him Lucky.

He became my perfect, sentient companion. He doesn't judge. He doesn't care about my past. His snoring soothes me.

Perfection is overrated. Lucky taught me how to love my sad-ass, flawed self—because *he* sure does.

And that's enough for me.

At last.

60. FOR MOTHER, WITH LOVE AND ESSENTIAL LA MER CRÈME DE LA MER

My mother's end began with a fall.

She barely made a sound when she hit the gold-flecked linoleum—her frail, 86-year-old frame composed of skin, bones, and pure determination.

Always the sartorial exemplar, she treated her cane like a festive accessory, not a tool to prevent catastrophic injury. It was adorned with bells and silver, lit up at night, and she wielded it like a cheerleader's baton.

There was no cheering the day she fell. Only the agonized scream that followed—a sound I'd never heard from her before. It was a warning shot. The beginning of the end.

Ever the dutiful daughter, I called her doctor immediately. He refused to prescribe anything for her excruciating back pain, concerned she'd become *addicted.* I protested. No luck. Maybe he sensed the desperation in my voice. Or maybe *she* had tipped him off about her pill-friendly daughter.

As any resourceful addict will tell you, I did the next wrong thing. I called a more … understanding doctor. He promptly wrote a script for 100 Vicodin "for my mother." My kind of man. She took (most of) them as prescribed and—unlike me—never got addicted.

Six months after that fall—we still don't know if she tripped or simply collapsed—she was diagnosed with lung cancer. Her new doctor practically dragooned her into lung surgery, threatening to fire her if she didn't comply. Another gem in the long line of compassionate medical professionals I've known. She survived the surgery—cancer-free—only to be told she had lymphoma.

When informed she'd need chemotherapy, she blinked and asked, "What's that?" She thought it was a card game, like Canasta.

"It's not a card game, Ma," I told her. "It's more of an endgame."

After that, she sat alone in her lavish condo, crossing off the days like a prisoner on death row. I visited when I could. Even then, she begged me to stay out of her kitchen. I was 58 years old, so that wasn't a problem. During one visit, she leaned in and whispered, "I want to die."

I encouraged her to share that with the doctor. She was in hospice the next day. She didn't know what hospice was either—but she was delighted to learn the Depends were free.

Eleven days later, she was gone.

Before she passed, she asked, “Was I a good mother?”

“The best,” I lied.

As a recovering addict, her Ativan and morphine were tempting. But recovery had taught me what to do: flush the stash, eat a doughnut instead.

I was far from an ideal daughter—as demonstrated by the fact that I *did* steal two jars of her beloved La Mer moisturizer after gently applying one final layer to her face, right before her last breath. A proper sendoff. She would’ve approved. Thanked me, even.

Because … priorities.

Hers.

61. THE PHONE CALL

In all 77 years of my father's life, I received only one phone call from him. He called to tell me he wouldn't be able to visit me in the hospital while I was being treated for cancer—he had a business meeting.

If I'm being honest, I didn't want him to visit. I was afraid of him.

Was it because of that time he pushed me to the floor and kicked me in the ribs while my mother watched? No. That wasn't what made me fear him. It was his silence—the kind that said: *Don't bother me.*

That silence made me feel unwanted. Unloved.

The phone call was just another reminder that I was a burden. His business meeting mattered more than his daughter with bladder cancer on the eve of her surgery.

Is it any wonder I turned to drugs to quiet that deafening silence?

62. APPLES AND TREES, UNADDRESSED

According to AI:

Intergenerational trauma, also known as transgenerational trauma, refers to the transmission of trauma's effects across generations. It can manifest as mental health issues, physical health problems, and behavioral patterns in descendants of those who experienced trauma. Studies show that trauma, especially when unaddressed, can significantly impact future generations.

My father's mother, Grandma Charna, died when my dad, Paul Kodimer, was just 14 years old. By all accounts, he loved her.

On the flip side, my father's father, who we called Grandpa Mac, was a real piece of work. After Grandma

Charna died, Grandpa Mac went on to marry five women in rote succession. Grief was not in his vocabulary. Neither was gratitude.

When my father turned 18, Grandpa Mac unceremoniously locked him and his spare possessions out of their apartment, making Paul homeless on the cusp of adulthood.

Against all odds, my father made his way in the world, became wildly successful and went on to financially support Grandpa Mac for decades. This did not prevent Grandpa Mac from eventually becoming a crossing guard late in life (his vocational zenith), just as it did not prevent him from suing my father for "insufficient financial support." As there was no legal basis whatsoever for his spurious claim, the case was thrown out. Paul, for reasons understood by no one, continued to send his father money, expecting nothing in return.

Grandpa Mac eventually died of complications from diabetes. My father initially refused to go to his funeral; my mother convinced him to make an appearance. Paul was not easily persuaded, so this was no small feat. Soon after the burial, he gave my mother a mammoth diamond ring. Go figure. Maybe he used the money he would have spent on the ungrateful ass who was his father to prove something—to send a message: *See dad, you can kick me out of your apartment, and I can still live a large life!*

Maybe my dad was the Large Yam OG. I like to think it was me, but apples don't fall far from the tree.

To that end, my father was not altogether different from his father. Like Grandpa Mac, Paul Kodimer excommunicated his only son after my brother committed the grievous mortal sin of marrying an Asian woman. *Poof* went their relationship. There's a lot about my father that I will never understand or accept, including the reality that I was similarly disowned by him when my addiction proved unworkable and inconvenient to my parents.

Incredibly, the Kodimer ancestral folk story seems quaint compared to my mother's family lore.

We called my mother's father Grandpa Joe. He was a cruel and terse man.

After being one of the few Jews to enlist in the Marines, Grandpa Joe returned home triumphant, only to carry on his Marine mentality as a parenting modality. Why not treat the children as wee conscripts? Why not shame and destroy them emotionally, break them down to build them up? Why not do the same to his wife and mother of those children?

He criticized my Aunt Blossom by repeatedly commenting on how fat she was. This, of course, traumatized my aunt for the rest of her life. She became an alcoholic and compulsive overeater, avoiding her feelings and covering up the pain with substance abuse and food. That pattern rings a bell. While I followed in her footsteps for the most part, I digressed when I got sober.

My mother undoubtedly heard her father fat-shaming her sister and vowed to please him, earn his love, by becoming a first-rate restrictive anorexic. The jury is out as to whether she ever won over her militant patriarch.

Another of my mother's sisters became so severely depressed that she took her own life when she was in her 20s. Who knows how Joe scrambled her eggs, but I'm certain he did. I hope, in his life and afterlife, he was and is plagued with guilt.

My mother's mother, Grandma Mary, threatened her lifelong draconian husband with divorce on the regular. His perpetual abusiveness and her perennial attempts to leave did not a happy marriage make. Of all my dysfunctional grandparents, I was closest to Grandma Mary. She was in and of my life, especially during the holidays, but I would not describe our connection as strong. In hindsight, this makes me sad. Every kid should have a grandparent with whom they feel safe, seen, loved.

For the record, Grandma Mary was also the recipient of my father's financial support until her death at 90-something.

All this is to say that my parents were genetically doomed. Our family, having seamlessly handed off the baton of intergenerational trauma, won the relay.

I understand now that without the benefit of healthy role models, my parents did not have or learn the skills necessary to be loving, nurturing parents. This explains but does not excuse their non-parenting, unique brand of dysfunction. I have suffered greatly because of their ignorance.

But now, with a deeper understanding of my family background, I know that *you can't give what you never had if you don't do the work.*

Can I really blame them? No one in their generation did the work, right?

As to my mother, with all her idiosyncrasies, forgiveness came more easily.

With my father, though, I'm still working on it, 80 years later. He should have known better, loved better. I carry that anger and pain within just as I carry their DNA, their marrow, in my bones and soul.

63. LIKE FATHER (AND MOTHER?), LIKE DAUGHTER

In the advanced stages of my father's Parkinson's disease, he was bedridden. He was hospitalized more than 50 times in five years. Not an exaggeration. It was brutal for all involved.

Watching this lion of industry—a man who built a grocery empire—reduced to a shell of himself was devastating. For him, it was worse, but you'd never have known it. He never complained.

By the end, he had round-the-clock caregivers whose main task was to roll him over to relieve his pain. Blind from diabetes, he listened to talk radio for company. He could no longer eat solid food, but he still enjoyed sucking on popsicles until a feeding tube became necessary. Through it all, he didn't want to die. Strident and stubborn to the core, he was determined to squeeze every drop of joy out of life.

He died alone in a hospital bed. Pneumonia.

I visited him often. I saw what Parkinson's could do. What I didn't realize then: I was looking at my own future.

Six years before my diagnosis, my right index finger started to twitch. I told no one. Not my cat, not my caregivers. This was my secret.

I can live with this. No problem, I thought.

But then my writing got harder—my hand tensed and shook. I stuffed the truth down per usual. When my balance faltered and it was no longer safe to live alone, I hired full-time help. Just like Dad. 24/7 care.

I got a chariot. Some call it a walker, which I find a little pedestrian—mine is regal.

As DNA would have it, I am my mother's daughter in some ways.

These days, medication helps keep some symptoms at bay. Others, not so much. Parkinson's, as I've come to learn, isn't just about tremors. (If you've seen Harrison Ford in *Shrinking*, you know.) It's so much more.

It robs you of *you*.

The Parkinson's menu is varied and unwelcome: mild auditory and visual hallucinations. Daily nausea and persistent reflux. Deep depression and chronic insomnia—a recipe for total energy depletion. The kicker? A chronic UTI that just might be what puts me six feet under.

Recently, that very thing landed me in the hospital with sepsis.

Like my father, I wake up each day unsure which symptoms will dictate my hours. The difference? He chased joy until the bitter end. Me? Some days I do. Other days, I'm more resigned—more like dear Mother.

Still, I can say this with certainty: the life I've lived, between birth and death, has been uniquely mine.

And in the end, somehow, I found my way back to them.

EPILOGUE

Since relocating to Northern California, my previously hopeless mindset has shifted significantly. Having signed a new lease on life here, I finally gave myself permission to be happy.

Also, I now buy large yams. I eat them skin and all. They are my favorite food (if we aren't counting the cookies and cupcakes I can no longer eat). When I pick one up at Mill Valley Market, I remember the restricted life of poor Mother who knew only small potatoes.

And I smile.

No more small potatoes for this strong woman.

For those of you who read this book and are guilty of small potato practices I say … RISE UP. Throw them away.

Don't overwhelm yourself. Start with one large yam. Let it represent a new chapter and a new you.

The only person standing between you and your freedom to choose the life you deserve (*aka* the big yam you really want) is not your mother, your enabler, your frenemy or your naysayer. It's you. Tear down your walls and let people in. While the past may be prologue, it cannot define all of you.

Let you shine.

POWER to you and your big yam too!

ACKNOWLEDGMENTS

Parkinson's disease has made me acutely aware of the beauty in daily, minor miracles—but it's the people in my life for whom I am most deeply grateful. Every damn day, I give thanks for this simple, monumental truth: I have my wild, loyal, deeply human crew—my chosen family of origin. Perfectly imperfect.

And I love every one of them.

To Gina, my ghostwriter and editor extraordinaire. Couldn't ask for a better partner.

To Dana, my gifted, superlative therapist. She can bring a horse to water and make him drink.

To Nancy, who's torn between a lettuce leaf and a candy bar. A lovable perfectionist, she claims to be a vegetarian, but we know better.

To Karen, an opinionated talker with a big heart.

To Whender, my right-and-left-hand man. A complicated person, whom I love dearly. I wouldn't be here without him. No part of my life would function—let alone flourish—without him.

To Lisa. Friendship is costly, my sleeping buddy. Lisa is under the charming delusion that she knows everything about me, including when I should go to bed or the bathroom. Adorable. She also makes the best oatmeal in the county, and I'm forever grateful for her steady presence.

To Barbara, who didn't know I was writing this book but always knew I could.

To Ann, my very favorite cousin and pal. An intimate relationship.

To Lynn, a gentle soul.

To Bobby, who deals with pain like no one I know.

To Lucky, the wonder dog and a gift from the heavens.

To Paula, my Parkinson's buddy who always included me and made me feel special.

To my brother, a work in progress. I always wished we were closer and that you were more available. Now that you are right there by phone, though, I'm grateful.

To my Saturday AA sober sisters meeting, from whom I learn my lessons.

To Colleen, a special sponsor.

To Eleanor, my surrogate mother who taught me to hug.

To Rosa, my fearless rehab housekeeper.

To the staff at Insalata's, especially Dawn, Milan and Mariett, who fed me and loved me through some of my darkest hours.

To Mrs. See's for making candy.

To the readers of this book who might laugh and cry with me.

To Wendy. We shared our misery together.

To Ana, my Brazilian charm. A tireless worker who holds my hand when I need to feel loved.

To Erin, a whiz with all things social media and tech. Thank you. My hope for you is this: that you, like me, someday realize your worth.

To Susan, caregiver par excellence. She rubs my back, hugs me tight, and tells me how to live my life. Could a gal ask for anything more?

To Joyce, wherever you are. Thank you for my first year.

To Miss Baron, who gave me my first gold star and changed my life.

To Paul and Dorothy Kodimer, my parents, who didn't make me who I am today—I forgive you!

ABOUT THE AUTHOR

Born in LA on Valentine's Day 1945 to Paul and Dorothy Kodimer, Charlene has a brother named Charles, as her mother's imagination was limited.

She was born and raised in Cheviot Hills, a suburb of Los Angeles.

Charlene went to Berkeley and UCLA, majoring in English Literature, before getting her master's degree in learning disabilities at Cal State University, Northridge. She taught special needs students at Fernald, a former school and research center at UCLA.

She then took a sabbatical as a taste tester for the pharmaceutical industry for about 20 years. She got sober (the first time) in 1983.

Even while sober, life was not a rose garden. She struggled with major depression which consumed many years of her life.

In her 60s, she obtained her second master's degree, this time in psychology, at Phillips Graduate University.

An avid advocate of therapy and medication, she was sober (again) for 30 years before relapsing (again). Like many addicts, she self-medicated to cope with her mental illness and to ease the pain of depression.

Through a synchronistic suggestion, she was encouraged to go rehab in Northern California.

In 2017, as she drove across the Golden Gate Bridge into Marin County, a little voice inside her said *I want to live here*. She listened and it has changed her life.

With eight years of sobriety under her belt as this book launches, she is also the proud creator of *The Coloring Diva*, a program to foster creativity and reduce anxiety for folks in disadvantaged communities. While her recent Parkinson’s diagnosis put her passion project on pause, she continues to be known as The Donut Queen at AA meetings, a notch above her former role as The Snack Lady. She gives back to her community often, especially during the holidays.

This book is her first attempt to put Parkinson's behind her and get on with her Bigass Yam Life.

COMING SOON!

HOW THE YAM FOUND HER VOICE:
LIVING YOUR BEST, LARGE LIFE

By Charlene Kodimer
with Gina Raith

Yes, that's a yam!

www.ingramcontent.com/pod-product-compliance
Lightning Source LLC
LaVergne TN
LVHW020714110826
845149LV00012B/2258